Praise for *A Widow's G*

"This is a very valuable and practical guide [...] her husband due to an untimely death. Kristin Meekhof's journey is both inspiring and courageous and something we can all learn from."

—*Deepak Chopra, MD, FACP*

"A wonderful balance of practical knowledge and inspiring advice that will give its readers a sense of peace and hope. I would have definitely appreciated a book like this when I first became widowed."

—*Amy Morin, LCSW, Bestselling Author of* 13 Things Mentally Strong People Don't Do

"[An] inspiring and insightful book to help guide widows through their grief. This book is by an Architect of Change, for all of us who must deal with grief."

—*Maria Shriver*

"Kristin Meekhof's book strikes a perfect balance between practical guidelines and compassionate wisdom for all seeking guidance following the often overwhelming loss of a spouse. It's the perfect everyday companion for readers as they follow their own life journey toward a 'new normal.'"

—*Dianne Gray, president, Elisabeth Kübler-Ross Foundation*

"This guide is an incredible resource for anyone in need of healing after losing their spouse. With Kristin Meekhof's book, recent widows can gain the tools and courage they need to carry on."

—*Michelle King Robson, president, EmpowHER*

"Finally a book that offers women who are new to widowhood a solid blueprint and empowering game plan while facing life's greatest challenge. This book offers supportive comfort to widows as they find hope again and most importantly, the healing needed to recreate their life. I wished I had this book when I became widowed many years ago. A light in the darkness of a widow's journey."

—*Carolyn Moor, founder, Modern Widows Club*

"One of the few things we know without certainty about life is that, in life, we never know. *A Widow's Guide to Healing* is that rare gem, a practical guide that makes the unthinkable bearable, the painful

manageable, and the road to healing a little brighter. You will be hard-pressed to find a better guide on growth in the aftermath of loss."
        —*Lee Daniel Kravetz, author of* Supersurvivors: The
                Surprising Link between Suffering and Success

"The most important quandaries bereavement poses—some with lifelong import—must be faced while widows are still reeling from emotional trauma. Or must they? Meekhof and Windell help vulnerable readers sort what can be put off and what must be done— and where to get help doing either. Had this guide been available back when I was rushing to extricate myself from the havoc left by my husband's death, their financial advice alone would have saved me substantial sums from which my children would have benefitted."
        —*Kathryn Craft, author of* The Far End of Happy

"This is the book that whispers in your ear everything you need to know...that you can't believe you need to know. It's all the things people are trying to tell you, when you want to hear it least... But more importantly, you hear it from other women who 'get it.' Kristin Meekhof provides a gentle and hopeful guide as you deal with the dark days. This is the book that will help you carry on despite the unbearable fog to find your inner confidence again. I wish I had this book to help me when my husband died."
        —*Susan Toffler, media strategist and widow*

"This is a book that should be essential reading for every woman struggling to make sense of life after the death of a husband. I recommend this book because it is highly accessible and will surely improve the lives of many widows and those who help widows."
        —*Lord Loomba, CBE, founder and chairman
                trustee of The Loomba Foundation*

"This book is a valuable resource for people within the medical profession to better understand hospice, palliative care, and death from a family perspective. When death does occur, this book can serve as a resource for providers as they guide widows and families through their grief."
        —*Gary D. Hammer, MD, PhD, Millie Schembechler Professor
        of Adrenal Cancer, University of Michigan, Director—Endocrine
                Oncology Program, Director—Center for Organogenesis*

a widow's guide to healing

Gentle Support and Advice for the First 5 Years

Kristin Meekhof, LMSW
James Windell, MA

sourcebooks

To all of the widows who generously shared
their stories. And to the memory of my beloved
husband, Roy; my courageous father, James
Vande Vusse; and my loving grandparents,
Ann and Howard Vande Vusse.
—KM

To my patient, understanding wife, Jane, who I hope
doesn't need this book for a long, long time.
—JW

Published by Sourcebooks, Inc.
P.O. Box 4410, Naperville, Illinois 60567-4410
(630) 961-3900
Fax: (630) 961-2168
www.sourcebooks.com

Library of Congress Cataloging-in-Publication Data

Meekhof, Kristin.
  A widow's guide to healing : gentle support and advice for the first 5 years / Kristin Meekhof, James Windell.
    pages cm
  1. Widowhood. 2. Widows--Life skills guides. 3. Adjustment (Psychology) I. Windell, James. II. Title.
  HQ1058.M44 2015
                        2015013013

Printed and bound in the Unites States of America.

VP 10 9 8 7 6 5 4 3 2 1

contents

introduction
feeling less alone

A NOTE FROM KRISTIN MEEKHOF

YOU MAY HAVE FOUND MY BOOK BECAUSE YOUR SPOUSE DIED OR because someone near and dear to you just lost her spouse. Either way, I hope this book will give you solace—and more importantly, hope. Though I don't know what circumstances led to your partner's death, I know that you probably feel no one can relate to your pain. I've been there myself. When I was thirty-three, my husband died unexpectedly. Although I have an undergraduate degree in psychology and a master's degree in clinical social work, little prepared me for my role as a caregiver when Roy was diagnosed with a rare form of cancer and passed away after a brief but valiant battle against it. But while I thought I wasn't prepared to be a caregiver, I quickly realized I was *definitely* not prepared to be a widow when he passed away. Suddenly, I was alone, scared, and filled with a deep sadness I thought would never end. As we didn't have any children together, I endured many unbearably long evenings where silence was the only thing filling my home. What kept playing over and over in my mind was that I was going to have to start over from scratch and I would have to cope with overwhelming challenges like anxiety and social isolation.

At the time, I was living in Michigan, and I remember going to bookstore after bookstore, buying whatever books I could find about grief and loss. In my mind, I knew there had to be a book that would tell me how I was going to get through everything I was facing. There are lots of these types of books, and I've read an overabundance of them. Yet none of them were quite what I was looking for. I wanted a book that spoke to me about what to expect as a widow, what I would feel not only the first year after my husband died, but also several years following his funeral.

I knew what it was like to experience grief—after all, my father had passed away when I was five. But this time, when I lost my beloved husband, it was different. Everything was darker. I soon discovered what all widows learn: at the very moment you are stripped of your life partner and left numb and grieving, you must make crucial decisions that will affect the rest of your life. Finances, family alliances, estates, legal matters, sudden single parenthood, career changes—widows are in no mental state to grapple with these challenges, and yet they must. They need a blueprint that spells out exactly what to do. But nothing like this existed.

My coauthor, psychologist James Windell, and I had worked together before Roy's death, and Roy and I had spent time together with James and his wife outside of work. After I lost Roy, James and I began talking about a book for widows. We talked about how losing a spouse is a nearly universal experience, and yet it leaves every widow feeling utterly alone. But given the myriad grief guides out there, what kind of book could we write that would offer something new and hopeful?

Initially, we were stumped. Since my husband's death, I have rebuilt my life and dedicated a large part of it to writing about widowhood. In addition to my column about transformation through loss and healthy living on the *Huffington Post*, I contribute to various other websites and host my own site dedicated to helping widows. Feedback from widows and from readers on the *Huffington Post* convinced both of us that widows need a different kind of book, one that helps them through the practical challenges of widowhood while providing comfort and advice from other widows who have survived the ordeal themselves. Over months of talking, the concept and the vision of this book slowly came together.

It became the blueprint I'd been looking for since my own husband had passed away.

What we decided was that this book should offer a gentle guiding hand to the widow struggling with fresh grief and then walk her through the difficult first years of widowhood. But beyond that, we agreed, widows need to know that grief knows no particular time line, and that the process can be a long one—sometimes lasting five or six years or more. However, right from the beginning of the book, our focus is on steering widows through the agonizing weeks after a spouse's death and then into the longer term. The book provides detailed, week-by-week to-do lists of vital tasks to take care of in the first month, when new widows are typically shell-shocked and mentally foggy. It also tackles difficult situations and issues that widows often don't even think about until they find themselves in those situations: being a widow in the workplace, being a sudden single parent, dealing with in-laws and extended family, and so on. With honesty and compassion, we try to describe the range of experiences a widow will face after the loss of a spouse.

On top of that, we've included snippets from the lives and experiences of other real widows as well as practical advice on what to expect and how to manage in the first days, weeks, months, and years after loss. While you may not know the widows in these pages, we hope that each of their voices will come across as a friend talking to you—a friend who unfortunately understands what you are going through, your feelings about your loss, your stressors, and your fears. Our goal is that reading this book will make you feel less alone, that it will help you get back on your feet and begin to heal, and that you may gain some additional life knowledge that will help you for years down the road.

Since I faced the same loss you are going through, I use my voice to describe some of the things I experienced. When you see the pronoun "I," you will know that this is my voice. There are times when Jim, as a psychologist, writes, and we try to make it clear that he is the writer of these passages. My personal reflections and Jim's perspective and analysis are joined by the voices of over one hundred widows ages twenty-five to eighty, whom we interviewed about their experiences, and whose memories and insights provide comfort and support. We believe that the sisterhood in these pages will assure you that you are not alone and that you can survive this terrible loss. By the end of the book, you will understand how to get your bearings, take control of your life, and create a game plan for the coming years.

Above all, I hope you will see how widows of various ages from all different educational, economic, and family backgrounds were able to transform their loss into something of meaning and beauty. You can do the same, and you will.

HOW TO USE THIS BOOK

One of the main purposes of our book is to give you practical advice, so we have commissioned experts from a variety of fields to discuss the hurdles that lie ahead. Some of the issues may be totally unfamiliar to you. For example, most of us have never had to deal with settling an estate, coping with inheritance taxes, and trying to decipher complex medical bills or make decisions concerning a deceased spouse's business affairs. Other important areas, such as solo parenting, employment, and managing personal relationships, are also addressed.

The issues you have to face and deal with as a widow will be daunting at times. Primarily because you are very likely to be vulnerable, disoriented, and emotionally exhausted—particularly in the weeks and months following your loss. That means you risk making impulsive or desperate decisions that can have devastating consequences. In clear, encouraging language, we provide a reasonable road map while pointing out possible hazards.

This book is unique in the sense that you don't need to read the chapters in order. In fact, you may skip over entire chapters that you don't feel pertain to you at the present time. Go ahead and read the ones that address your most urgent issues.

In Chapter One, we discuss what you will have to deal with in the first few weeks and months. But beyond pointing out what you will face, we offer important to-do lists and advice in Chapter Two about identifying and coping with the necessities and the urgencies, as well as what you can put off until later. This is especially useful if you're feeling overwhelmed. In Chapter Three, we introduce you to the legal system that surrounds death and loss in this country and discuss complicated issues like estate taxes and wills. We also show you how you can successfully navigate challenges like the probate court and legal maze on your own, and discuss when to consult a legal professional to help you work through any legal questions or concerns.

Chapter Four describes the various challenges you may face if you have children you are still raising. It's not easy being a solo parent—especially when you weren't expecting to be one!—but we offer various strategies to help you navigate sticky issues such as talking to your child (or children) about the death of their other parent, discipline as a solo parent, and how to handle those future awkward moments—when your child asks questions about their other parent, when that father-daughter dance comes up at school, and when you start to date or plan to remarry.

In Chapter Five, we discuss the challenges to expect when dealing with friends and family after your loss. Things change when your spouse dies. Your close friends and your family may be a wonderful source of support. And you may actually achieve greater closeness with some relatives. But there may also be friction, and sometimes hostilities even develop. Friends, coworkers, and even family members can get weird or awkward about addressing or discussing your loss or may not be sure how to approach your new status as a widow. In addition, it is often difficult to keep your coupled friends when you are no longer part of a couple. This chapter offers a straightforward look at possible problem areas and advice on how to navigate them, while also providing comfort and support.

Many widows will find Chapter Six a very valuable chapter as we walk you through the various financial questions and concerns you will likely face. These range from trying to find all the assets and bills (if your spouse always handled the money) to whether you need a financial planner and how to find the right financial planner for you.

In Chapter Seven, we cover work and careers. With the sage advice of career counselors and employment experts, we offer advice and recommendations related to getting a job (if you have been out of the job market for a long time) or changing careers. We even talk about questions you may face if you are returning to work after taking a short break for grief and recovery, and, of course, we suggest ways to respond to the too-personal and the frankly inappropriate questions you may encounter.

In interviewing over one hundred widows, we learned valuable things about the challenges widows encounter. We found that widows are eager to share the lessons grief has taught them. In Chapter Eight, we cover a great many things widows come to learn that they can pass on to you. Other widows talk about such matters as unhappy marriages and caring for a terminally ill spouse—and the guilt that results. We openly discuss forgiveness and other challenges you might never anticipate you would have to face.

Our last chapter is "Your Game Plan." This chapter is filled with charts, to-do lists, checklists, and tables that help you handle all sorts of situations widows have to deal with from week one to year five or beyond. This chapter will give you practical tools for many different aspects of your life: from helping you ask for help, to creating a budget, to deciding whether you can afford to stay in your home, and much more.

Throughout the book, we try to offer comfort and reassurance. At the same time, we are realistic about the rigors of coping after the death of your partner. We offer our own opinions as well as the guidance of experts to help you through a life passage that almost a million women in the United States experience each year. Along with our real-world advice, we present quotes from widows from a variety of backgrounds. All of this makes the book a unique resource for widows of any age. We sincerely hope that this book brings you the comfort and guidance you seek.

chapter one

the 411 on surviving the first month

"MS. MEEKHOF?"

"Yes?"

"I'm John Fredrick, the hospice care specialist, calling to see how you're doing."

"I'm fine."

"There are a lot of things hospice can offer you in your time of loss…"

"I can't talk now. It's not the best time."

I'm standing alone in my small galley kitchen, staring at the wall. Did I said good-bye or just hang up? I'm not sure.

I glance over at my oblong dining room table, which seats six and now is home to various stacks of paper. To anyone else it would look chaotic, but I've spent a lot of time organizing all these papers into piles according to subject, like a student collecting notes before finals week. These are my piles: hospice, inpatient, outpatient, funeral. Each has a different folder with it, and I'm proud of myself for being able to sort through all this.

I feel like I should be doing something, so I walk to the table and pick up the purple folder labeled "Hospice." I look over each paper, one by one. A light pink receipt from the University of Michigan Hospital reads, "Pickup Ticket—adult walker." I used this ticket to get the walker because hospice told me my husband Roy could use it.

I glance at the bottom of the form and see my signature, "Kris Meekhof." I've never signed anything "Kris." It's always Kristin. But that was before my world fell apart. I look closely again. It is definitely my handwriting, although I don't remember signing the form.

I'm searching my memory, trying hard to recall when I signed this. Was Roy in the car? Did I run in, sign it, and leave? How did I get the walker into the car? I just can't remember. I can visualize the pickup dock—it had a long ramp that I walked up, and inside there was a stairway. I'm trying to reconstruct the rest of that moment. It's not coming back.

Now I'm trembling. My heart is racing and tears are welling in my eyes. I let the pickup form and the folder slip out of my hand, onto the table. I walk away, leaving the purple folder open.

The tears are really flowing now. But something is coming back to me as I look out the window. A snippet returns. I remember I tossed the walker into the back hatch of our black Volvo station wagon and Roy said, "Careful with that."

Another memory surfaces. Earlier that afternoon we were in a small waiting room, between radiation appointments. The radiation was palliative, not actual treatment. I knew Roy was going to die. As we sat quietly, Roy said, "I have absolutely no fear of dying. I just don't want to leave you behind."

Two weeks after picking up that walker, he died and I was left behind.

These moments can still catch me off guard and stop my heart: a stranger's telephone call, a medical statement, a signature. When that happens, I may be blindsided by sadness, but I can usually collect myself. Back then, though, I wasn't handling things very well. My mind was stuck on just three words: *my husband died.*

....

When I lost my husband Roy, it was as if I'd entered another universe. I wasn't only grief stricken, I was disoriented, terrified, and completely at a loss as to what I was supposed to do next. Although I wasn't on any medication, I felt like I was in a coma. I could hear what was going on, my body was present, but my mind was elsewhere.

There were issues I had to deal with immediately, decisions that had to be made, but I had no experience with this thing…widowhood. *This was not my life.* I needed a blueprint for how to survive the next week, the next month, and the next year.

As we mentioned in the introduction, this is why we wrote this book—to give you a blueprint. This chapter will tell you what you'll need to deal with in the first few weeks after your partner's passing. We'll provide detailed guidelines, so you won't have to feel like you're all alone. If you do these tasks one by one, and know who to ask for help, you can manage it. This will be a terribly difficult few weeks, but you can and will get through it.

IT'S NORMAL TO BE IN A FOG

No one thinks clearly after a tremendous loss like the one you have just experienced. For me, it felt like my stomach was perpetually churning and the skin on my head was pulled too tight. When my coauthor, Jim, and I interviewed people about the first days and weeks of widowhood, they said similar things: "I was in a fog." "I felt like I was moving underwater." "It felt like there was a cement block on my head."

WHAT WIDOWS SAID

I had periods of weakness and quivering sensations. I had gone to the doctor for something else and mentioned that I was having these strange sensations and he told me that these were very common feelings and that they would eventually pass (which they did), but he said there was really nothing to do for them.

—BARBARA, 64

I had never experienced panic attacks prior to my husband's death. Not only that, my sleep was greatly impacted. I couldn't go to sleep at night until I was exhausted. Then, with only a couple of hours sleep, I was not functioning well at work. I couldn't concentrate. Then, I developed fears. I was afraid I would die. I experienced fears about almost everything—going to the dentist, driving at night, getting lost. I actually had to get a Valium prescription in order to cope on a day-to-day basis.

—LAURA, 55

After I learned about my husband's death, I just went numb. Shock is an amazing function of the human brain. It protects you from absorbing too much information but allows you to still speak, move your limbs, and breathe. Your brain only lets in what you can handle, in small or sometimes large doses, depending on your capability to accept the loss. But in the beginning, I was at about zero. Everything was too much for me to take in.

—EVELYN, 42

I was shaking for two weeks. I couldn't write my name. I couldn't eat. I was in a daze...walking around like a zombie. I was stunned...numb... I didn't feel anything... But I organized myself. I knew I had to do things. I made a list of fifteen or twenty things I had to do. But it was hard going to the bank and closing out his accounts.

—ELLEN, 57

In my sister's arms that night, I experienced what she described as labor pains from grief. I sounded like I was giving birth, but instead of having a new life be the reward, there was to be no happy ending. The only reason I got out of bed was to feed my beagles. I couldn't have people around because when a wave of grief would come over me, my throat would fill up so much that I would throw up. This went on for four months until a good friend gently suggested I go on some sort of medication. But I was afraid to do this.

—DELIAH, 41

Like these new widows, you may not be able to think as clearly as you usually do—and as you will again in the future. For right now, your needs are simple. You need to get up and get dressed every day and then be guided toward whatever must be done. During the first few days, weeks, or, in some instances, months after the death of your spouse, you may not be able to recall whether you ate lunch or where you parked your car. You may have difficulty trying to find the words to complete a thought. Emotions and events may be foggy, and at times you may experience trancelike symptoms. We want to assure you that all of this is completely normal.

Communicating with other people can be a particular challenge during this time. You may feel as if you are talking underwater and they don't understand you. The funeral director hands you a box of your partner's belongings to go through; you wonder if he's trying to rob or trick you when he makes suggestions that will cost more money. A neighbor you hardly know appears at your door with a check for fifty dollars, saying, "For expenses—this is our custom." You are baffled. The only reason you answered the door is because you thought by some cosmic fluke it might be your partner standing there, waving a magic wand to bring you out of your nightmare, not a neighbor offering to help you pay for your own expenses.

You may start each morning by having a conversation with yourself, convincing yourself to get out of bed. You tell yourself, "Today I will do three things on my list… Where's my list? Wait, I don't have a list. What should be on the list? I don't even know." All of this is normal. You have not lost your mind. The important thing to know is that everyone who suffers a loss, expected or unexpected, is experiencing a significant trauma. As Megan, the wife of a man who committed suicide, said, "You go into robo-mode." She and other widows confessed, "I just wanted someone to tell me what to do next."

WHAT TO DO THE FIRST MONTH

If you're reading this book about widowhood, chances are you have already held a funeral or memorial service for your spouse or partner. (If you have not yet arranged the service and need guidance, please see the Resources section at the back of this book.) A week or more has probably passed, and with the funeral over, you're left standing in a very quiet house, shell-shocked. Friends and family ask what they can do to help, but you have no idea because you need help with every-thing. Although you are traumatized, by the second week certain practical matters must be attended to. We'll talk about long-term and ongoing financial arrangements in Chapter Six, but some aspects of your finances will need your attention right away. In addition to bills, insurance, and legal issues, there are concerns involving your job, your kids, their school…so many things to think about! But what do you tackle first?

In the following sections, you'll find weekly to-do lists to help you organize your tasks during this difficult, confusing first month. We strongly urge you to ask other people to help you, even with the seemingly easy things like opening a pile of neglected mail or compiling a list of people who need to be sent thank-you notes.

Weeks One and Two: Tasks That
Need Your Attention ASAP

1. **If you have moved, even temporarily, notify utilities, newspaper delivery, landlord, and the post office.** If you want your mail delivered to a new address, file that paperwork with your local post office branch. In many cities, this may be done online. This is a good task to ask a friend to do for you.

2. **Call your employer.** Your decisions about working will naturally depend on your financial resources as well as your state of mind. You may be ready to return to work, or you may need to take a few more days or weeks. Your company may allow you an extended unpaid leave of absence, or you may be able to use vacation and sick days to buy yourself a little more time before returning to the office. You'll need to discuss your options with your employer, your supervisor, or the HR department. In Chapter Seven, we will look at jobs, careers, and employment in greater detail.

WHAT WIDOWS SAID

I was fifty-one when my husband died and I couldn't wait to get back to work. I loved my job, and I needed to maintain a level of productivity in my life. In a sense I saw my job as benefiting others, and that was important to me. It helped me to keep a balance in my life.

—DIANNE, 76

There was a part of me that kept saying, "You have to stay away from the office in order to cope." But I needed the money if I was going to stay in my house. When I had used up all of my savings, I went back to

> work. This was four months after his death. I had to do that for financial reasons, but going back to work full-time saved me emotionally.
>
> —GLORIA, 49
>
> I knew it would be an emotional ordeal to go back to the office. I put it off as long as I could, but I finally went back. It was pretty much as I expected. Most people had heard my husband had died and they all wanted to talk to me. But that only lasted a couple of weeks, and then I could focus on the work. That was good for me.
>
> —ALEXIS, 36

3. **Pay bills—mortgage or rent, credit cards, utilities, and so on.** Although you may intend to move later, maintaining your financial obligations will give you more options. Check on all debts and installment payments, including credit cards. Some may carry insurance clauses that will cancel the debt. If there is to be a delay in meeting payments, consult with the company to request more time before the payments are due. Go to the bank and get statements for all your accounts, or access them online. If you have been living in crisis mode, you may have made purchases that you didn't document. Your statements will help you get on track. You will eventually want to bring a copy of the death certificate to the bank and change the names on the accounts, but if you're feeling too raw, it is not necessary to do this right now.

4. **Open your mail.** If you are unsure of what to do with it, just save it. Don't shred anything until you can review it later. If mail is piling up and you can't face it, ask a friend or family member to sort it for you and show you only the items that are important.

5. **Locate your spouse's will and notify your attorney (if you haven't already).** The will may designate an executor, and you

should discuss this with your attorney. In most states, a will must be admitted to probate before your partner's property can be distributed to you or other heirs. Probate is the court process by which the will is proved to be valid. The person in possession of the will, be it the wife, attorney, or someone else, must produce it. No one has the right to suppress a will. Statutes impose penalties for concealing or destroying a will or for failing to produce it within a specified time.

It is best to consult an attorney to handle this, but you can contact your county's probate court to ask questions. Just keep in mind that a will has no legal effect until it is probated. Filing the will should occur as soon as possible, or at least within thirty days of your spouse's death. In many states, the allowed amount of time is one month from the death of the individual. If you know that the person in possession of the will has not filed it, you may notify the court so that the court can compel the filing. Then the probate process can begin. If for some reason you are unable to file your spouse's will within thirty days, you must notify the probate court. Most courts give you some leeway, but don't assume anything—find out for certain if your court will. If you fail to file the will within thirty days, you can be compelled by the court to file the will or you can be cited by the court with the possibility of criminal penalties. If there is no will, see Chapter Three for an explanation of what to do.

6. **Contact your children's teachers and/or schools.** Call, email, or visit the school principal and your child's teacher (if your child is in elementary school) or the teachers or counselor (if your child is in middle or high school). You could also send a letter or email to people you think should have information about your child, such as a counselor, coach, or tutor. The purpose in contacting these people is to let them know how you want them to handle your child. Certainly, someone at school needs to know that your child has suffered a significant loss and that his or her behavior will probably reflect that. Unusual behaviors

could include withdrawal, lack of attention, crying, emotional outbursts, or being more clingy than usual with a teacher. In Chapter Four, you can read more about how to help your child cope with grief.

7. **Order death certificates.** The easiest way to get certified copies of your spouses's death certificate is to order them through the funeral home or mortuary within thirty days of the death. You should ask for at least ten copies because you will need one each time you change bank accounts, close out credit cards, or claim property or benefits that belonged to your spouse (which may include life insurance proceeds, Social Security benefits, and veterans' benefits). If you didn't do this within thirty days of the death of your partner, contact your county or state vital records office, where the death certificate should be on file.

8. **File for life insurance benefits.** Carefully check all the life and casualty insurance policies your partner had and apply for those that include death benefits. You will need copies of the death certificate to file for insurance benefits. If your partner was still working, you may need to talk to his employer or the human resources department to learn more about applying for death benefits.

Keep in mind that if you are the beneficiary of your spouse's life insurance policy, you must file a claim to receive your benefits—the payout is not automatic. Usually, it is a simple matter of calling your insurance agent or the insurance company, and then filling out the paperwork. Be sure to have a certified copy of the death certificate for each insurance company. As you look over the assets and important papers, you may find insurance benefits of which you were unaware, but to which you are entitled. These could include individually owned policies (which may be filed away in a safe deposit box or a file cabinet), group life insurance policies, which may have been issued through an employer, bank, or credit union; or accidental death and dismemberment policies, which may have been offered as part of a loan package or issued as a free benefit by a bank or credit union, or as a rider to an employer-issued insurance policy.

If you have an attorney, he or she may be helpful in this process, but your life insurance agent—the person who sold or serviced the insurance policy—may provide the most assistance in processing a life insurance claim. You also can contact the company's policyholder service department directly, but your agent (if you have one) may offer more support. For instance, you may be receiving a steady stream of bills at this time. The funeral expenses, hospital bills, and your spouse's outstanding debts can add up to a substantial sum—on top of all the regular household bills. Even if you expect money from one or more insurance policies or the estate settlement, it may not come in time to pay this month's bills. Your insurance agent can help you arrange for an advance or loan against the life insurance benefit due. If not, you may be able to borrow cash from a credit card account or open a home equity line of credit. If you have a financial professional, ask about your options and which fits best, given your investments and assets.

9. **File for Social Security Survivor Benefits for you and your children if they are under eighteen.** If your spouse was receiving Social Security, you must notify both the bank (if the Social Security checks are deposited directly into a checking or savings account) and the Social Security Administration. Social Security Form SSA-721, which might be available from the funeral home, must be filed with the Social Security Administration. You can go to the Social Security website (www.ssa.gov) for more information. If you need to sign your children up as dependents to receive Survivor Benefits, be sure to have a copy of the death certificate and their birth certificates. Widows are entitled to Survivor Benefits if they make less than a specific annual income. Go to www.socialsecurity.gov/survivorplan/howtoapply.htm for the most current information.

Week Three: Medical Bills, Unneeded Insurance Policies, Social Media, and Phone Calls

1. **Organize hospital, doctor, and other medical bills.** These are often totally confusing and indecipherable. You'll get multiple versions of medical bills, month after month, if you don't pay them within thirty days (and it is common to ignore the bills while dealing with a spouse's medical crisis or terminal illness). The bills are frequently incorrect; insurance companies generally will not notice or contest inaccurate bills. In our opinion, widows need some sort of professional help dealing with these bills. There are a few nonprofit organizations that will take a second look at medical bills and negotiate a lower rate. Personally, I remember a very costly scan being rejected by my insurance. I asked the doctor to write a letter to appeal it. Not only did he appeal it, he called the insurance company on my behalf. The bill was paid in full by the insurance company.

   Often, doctors' offices will work with you if you explain that your spouse has died and you are struggling. A widow we interviewed was left no life insurance and had huge debts because her husband had been out of work for years due to his illness. She called a few of the doctors' offices, swallowed her pride, and explained her financial situation. She was prepared to set up a payment arrangement but, much to her surprise, one of the physicians absorbed the entire balance. Two others lowered the balances and agreed to let her make payments over many months.

> After my husband passed away, I called our life insurance agent about his policy and she offered to come over and help me sort out the medical bills. I had been shoving them into a grocery bag the whole time he was sick. She straightened out the mess in one long afternoon.
>
> —RHONDA, 47

2. **Cancel insurance policies (such as your spouse's auto insurance) that you no longer need.** Paying out insurance premiums for policies you don't need is a waste of money, but first you need to make an inventory of all the insurance policies you both had. Then decide which ones need to be canceled. Here is another situation where a friend, an insurance agent, or a financial advisor might be very helpful, in organizing and then notifying the insurance companies to cancel the unwanted policies.

3. **Decide how to manage your partner's social media.** Social media is a very delicate issue. Some families prefer keeping their loved ones' accounts active because others will write messages on the pages. It's not necessary for you to make a statement on your partner's (or your own) social media sites, but it can be comforting to read others' memories of your spouse.

   You may not be aware of all the different social media sites your partner was using. However, if you know where he stored his passwords, you may be able to figure it out. Then you'll need to decide when or if to shut them down. For example, Eva, 51, decided not to cancel her husband's Facebook page right away. As she explained, "My husband took his life. I was devastated but also extremely angry and hurt that he did this to me and the kids. He was beloved in the community where he worked, but I didn't want to deal with anyone. His friends and colleagues used Facebook to express their love and appreciation for him, and that ended up really helping me get through it. We also posted photos of the memorial service on his Facebook page."

   In addition to social media, many people have their own websites for work or just for personal use. If your spouse was connecting to a great many people through such a website, you will have to make a decision about whether you want to maintain the website or close it down.

   You should be aware that there are many groups on Facebook for widows. Some of these are private, and others are open to any new widow. For more resources, see the Appendix at the back of this book, "Resources for Widows."

4. **Decide how to manage your incoming phone calls.** For new widows, caller ID is a godsend. There will be some people you need and want to talk to, and others you don't. Well-meaning friends may ask intrusive questions or want to dwell on things related to your partner that are upsetting, and these calls should go to voice mail. You are not required to discuss your partner, his death, or how you are coping. For many widows, it is utterly draining to talk endlessly about being alone or having cared for a dying spouse. In some cases, your partner's friends may want to call and commiserate or look to you for comfort—but it is not your duty to provide that, and certainly not at this early stage. You can reminisce with them later, if you want to.

Put your phone on silent mode when you don't want to hear it ring, and always check the caller ID before you answer. Never feel guilty about letting calls go to voice mail, and do not feel compelled to return calls unless they are urgent. Doing this will help you conserve the energy you'll need to function during these first weeks. If you end up feeling guilty about ignoring the callers, ask a friend (or several friends) to return the calls and relay a message for you.

What about your spouse's cell phone? You can ask a friend to put an outgoing message on it, you can simply ignore it, or you can stop service on it now or later. I kept my husband's cell phone line active for more than a month after he died. I loved being able to call it and hear his voice on the outgoing message. Some of my friends thought it was odd, but it made me feel better.

Week Four: Tasks That Should Be Done by the End of the First Month

1. **Prepare a list of people who need to receive acknowledgment of flowers, gifts, or condolences.** You may want to

send a note or handwritten card to everyone who attended the funeral or sent flowers. Asking a friend or relative to help might be especially useful for this task, which many widows tend to avoid.

2. **Change the names on joint bank accounts and other financial assets.** You may not have to change all joint accounts immediately, but at some point you will. For now, you should at least have a list of the accounts that will need to be changed. This can be time-consuming, and it's one of those tasks you could put on a list to have ready for friends who ask, "What can I do to help?" An older child—an adolescent or adult—could help with this too.

I found out that everything was in my husband's name. We had health insurance through a hospital where he worked before we moved to Baltimore. I didn't know I was supposed to contact them and reapply for health insurance after he died. No one told me, and the hospital just canceled the insurance. Then there were things like credit cards, cell phones, and car leases. I had to call all of these companies and reapply for accounts in my name. I would end up talking for hours on the phone with people, having to repeat the same story over and over and then having to send out multiple copies of the death certificate. I often felt like telling the story of his death to people made them not want to talk to me—so they would pass me off to others. The worst was dealing with the Department of Motor Vehicles. All I was doing was just trying to return the license plate from his leased car. When I went to the DMV with the license plate, I had to wait for my number to be called. Then I took the license plate to the counter and told the woman I wanted to return it. She said: "Ma'am, you are not the owner of the license plate. He must return it himself."

> Then, I got shifted to a supervisor, who couldn't seem to understand why he couldn't return it himself. No one said, "I'm sorry for your loss." This was something I wished someone else could have handled for me.
>
> —DEBRA, 55

When you're ready to face more stress, you can go to the bank in person. I remember calling our small local branch bank and being told that I needed to bring in a copy of the death certificate for the account to be changed. I hung up the phone, got in my car, and drove to the bank, expecting things to go smoothly. In the bank, I walked up to the counter and handed over the death certificate and my checkbook, because that's where the account number was listed. The bank employee looked at me. She seemed stunned and said, "I just saw your husband two weeks ago. What happened?" There were tears in this woman's eyes.

I had no idea that he had even gone to the bank, so I said, "He was here?"

"Yes, he said that he was getting treatment for cancer. He looked good."

I couldn't believe that my husband had told the bank employee this, but then I was interested in what else he said. I asked, "Did he say anything else?"

"No, he just said that he might not be in for a while," she said.

When I heard that, I broke down in tears. I grabbed the paperwork and turned my head. I remember saying, "I'm sorry." But I nearly ran over the customer standing behind me and didn't return to that bank for weeks. The account was left unchanged until I was ready to go back and try again. There's no way to entirely avoid being emotionally blindsided, but in that situation, having a friend along might have helped me pull myself together and finish the transaction.

SIX WAYS TO MAINTAIN YOUR SANITY IN THE FIRST MONTH AND BEYOND

Immediately after your spouse passed away, while you were planning the funeral, you may have had plenty of family members around to comfort and support you. Although you might have been in a state of shock, all the activity absorbed some of the grief, or at least directed your attention away from your own private sorrow. After the first week or so, the reality and weight of your situation will start to sink in. When I reached that point, I wanted to go to the doctor and get a prescription that would make me feel just like I had before Roy had died. Sadly, no one has the ability to restore us to feeling 100 percent again—only time can do that.

Meanwhile, friends, acquaintances, and business associates of your partner may be contacting you for various reasons. You may be approached by charitable organizations to which your spouse belonged, or you may want to remember your spouse through a foundation—make sure you hit the pause button and do not consider this for at least six months, when you have a better handle on your finances and emotions. You can tell anyone pressuring you to make quick decisions that you will let them know once things settle down.

In all your interactions during this time, keep these suggestions in mind:

1. **Don't try to be a people pleaser.** Sounds simple, right? But you may be on the receiving end of odd requests, bizarre questions, impractical demands, and unwanted advice. Be polite, but say no when needed to save yourself unnecessary stress, worry, or responsibility.
2. **Don't speak negatively about yourself.** Your self-esteem may take a plunge when you become a widow, and we will explore why in a later chapter. For now, you aren't doing yourself any favors by being down on yourself. Stop the inner critic. Treat yourself as you would your best friend in a similar situation. That means being kind to yourself.

3. **Trust your gut.** Normally, you may know how to respond to common comments or requests from others, but after your loss, you may second-guess yourself. Before responding (and potentially putting yourself in an awkward or difficult situation), stop and listen to your instincts. Your gut is probably correct. This can apply to so many parts of your life at this stage: friends and acquaintances offering unsolicited advice, people making suggestions that don't apply to you, salesmen trying to push a product on you, financial planners who get in touch with you, and even things your children may think is best for you. Trust yourself to know what's best for you.

4. **Breathe.** There will be moments when you are scared, uncertain, and terrified of what lies ahead. Remember to take deep breaths. It may sound cliché, but this simple action will help ground you. This is your therapy for now.

5. **Get a notebook, and each day write down what you did, to the best of your recollection.** There will be unusual phone calls and conversations that you may need to reference later. If they are all in your notebook, you can easily go back to the page and recall the date and conversation.

6. **Accept help.** You may not be sure what you're going to do with a pan of lasagna or a bag full of magazines, but saying yes to those who are reaching out is good for you. Maybe you like to think of yourself as Superwoman or Miss Independent, but this is one time when you need to give yourself a pass and put aside your do-it-yourself alter ego. Go ahead, say yes to that free haircut or the friend who wants to take you to dinner. You need the companionship, and it keeps valuable relationships intact. In fact, don't just accept help; get proactive about it. To learn how to do that, read on.

"Do You Need Any Help?" Yes, You Do!

Friends, family members, colleagues, members of your congregation, and other people you know will probably ask, "Is there anything I can do to help?" Your brain is likely too exhausted to come up with a concrete suggestion, so you reply, "Thanks, I'll let you know" or "Thanks so much, but I think I'm okay for now."

But yes, you do need help, even if you don't realize it. So now is the time to take advantage of these offers. Once you turn them down, they may not offer it again or they may not be willing to help when you really feel you are ready to accept it. There are a couple of ways you might respond to these offers. One is to write a list of all the tasks you need help with and carry it in your purse. When someone asks, pull out the list and say, "Thank you. That would be wonderful. I wrote this list of things that are a challenge for me right now. Would you be able to help with any of these?" Your list should include small and large tasks, so your friends can choose something that won't be too much of a burden for them. Their asking might seem like an empty gesture, but I've found that most people really mean it when they offer to help, and they'll be relieved to have something specific to do for you as they won't know what to offer to help you with.

Another way to get help is to ask people for specific things, with a time limit attached. That way, they won't feel like they are making an open-ended commitment that could be difficult to honor. Here is a list of tasks you might need assistance with right now; it will probably help you think of additional tasks. Next to any that apply to you, write down the names of people who might be good for the job:

- Bring dinner over one night a week for the next month. (It is okay to be specific. Go ahead and ask for a certain day; then you will know that on Tuesdays, for example, you can count on not having to make dinner.)
- Keep me supplied with the basics: coffee, cereal, paper towels, toilet paper. (These staples are essential, and it's easy to forget about them until you run out.)
- Help me write thank-you notes and cards.
- Pick up the ashes from the mortuary and keep them until I ask for them.
- Go on my partner's Facebook page (and Twitter, LinkedIn,

Pinterest, and so forth), and explain to his friends and contacts what has happened. Maintain the site for me for a month; then help me to decide whether to shut it down or continue it.

- Mow my lawn, rake the leaves, or shovel my walk or driveway.
- Help me contact our bank, credit card companies, or other creditors and explain what's happened, close out accounts, or change the names on the accounts.
- Take over my duties as soccer coach for two months.
- Babysit my children one afternoon or evening a week.
- Help me fix (fill in broken household item here: leaky faucet, sliding door that is stuck, etc.).
- Help me with my daughter's (or son's) college application and/or financial aid application.
- Listen to my voice mail messages and call back people relaying a message for me.
- Help me go to my husband's office and clean out his belongings.
- When I'm ready, help me go through the garage (or basement, attic, home office, etc.) and decide which of my husband's things to keep and which to get rid of.

There may be other responsibilities unique to your situation that you can add to your list. Bear in mind that it's easy to get blindsided when you are a new widow. Routine tasks you once did without a second thought may suddenly be difficult to manage on your own. Someday in the not-too-distant future, you'll be functioning more like your old self, but for the next few months, allow yourself to accept help.

WHAT WIDOWS SAID

A month after my husband died, I was still living in a fog. Actually, that started even before he died—knowing he was ill, but not knowing what was wrong. But I felt as though if I had to do something I didn't have enough energy. For instance, we had to do a new scholarship application for my youngest daughter, now that she was without a father. It was difficult finding the energy and the motivation to do this.

—KELLIE, 44

My sister wanted to help me get through this and she ended up doing everything for me. She contacted everyone and had all the accounts and addresses changed. She was an angel to do this.

—BIANCA, 45

THERAPY, GRIEF COUNSELING, AND WIDOW SUPPORT GROUPS

In the next chapter, we'll explore the various support systems that are available to widows, but by way of a preview, we want to mention them here. If things are too foggy and you don't feel like you are coping as well as you should be, reach out to professionals or support groups for temporary help. Many widows find the group sessions especially comforting and helpful. Being in these groups, which are usually run by counselors or psychologists, can reassure you that many of the emotions you're experiencing are normal and to be expected. However, if you don't feel comfortable sharing your feelings with a group of strangers, going to a private therapist for a brief time may help you get through the rough early phases of your grief. There are psychologists, counselors, social workers, and psychiatrists who specialize in helping people deal with grief and loss.

GRIEF COUNSELING FOR YOUR CHILDREN

If you have young children, they may be just as consumed with intense feelings of loss as you are. They are likely to express their feelings differently than you, but you need to talk to them frequently and give them a chance to express themselves, so you know how they are coping. If you are not sure how they are dealing with the death of their other parent, or if they display behaviors that concern you, by all means, see a child psychologist or a grief specialist who works with children. That's what Caroline, 31, did. "I think moms need to bring up conversations with their children about their dad as much as possible. I know I didn't do this enough because of my own emotions. But I did look for signs that my daughters were acting differently at school and other places. When I saw those signs, that's when I decided to find a grief therapist for them."

Since helping your children cope with their grief is such an extremely important issue, we are devoting a full chapter to that topic. Chapter Four will help you guide your children through their early grief, and it will answer the questions you are likely to have about the way children mourn the loss of a parent. In addition, we'll address how you can answer your children's questions, and we'll share some ways to encourage them to express their feelings.

CLEARING OUT YOUR PARTNER'S THINGS

We interviewed Wendy, 62, on the day she was going through her husband's belongings, almost two years after her beloved husband of forty-one years had died from a sudden heart attack. She was planning a garage sale to sell off his "stuff." As she said, "It is really difficult to go through his things. But it's his stuff. And I think it is time for it to go. You have mementos, and then you have things. I have the memories of all of our years together. I don't need to have the things."

Other widows acknowledged how difficult this was as well. But it doesn't have to be a somber occasion. Jim recalls that his mother went through his father's belongings just two days after the funeral.

"My sisters and our children were all in Florida, where my mom and dad lived, and my mother said it would be a good time to go through his personal things and let everyone take what they wanted to remember him by. As it turned out, we made a festive occasion of it. There were lots of photos, which we had fun looking at again, and there were many personal items—watches, rings, tie tacks, and so on—that everyone remembered him wearing. It brought back many memories and we could all reminisce about the good times and the long-forgotten events of past years. My mother shed a few tears, but then, we all did. However, it was fun too, and my mother enjoyed thinking back over the good years they had together."

Before Roy died, he was in hospice at home for ten days. There was a point just a few days before he died when my best friend told me that I would need to figure out what suit I wanted him buried in. She stood there while I selected the outfit. She then said, "Give me all of those other shirts but keep three of his favorites."

I wasn't ready for this. "What are you going to do with them?"

She looked at me while holding open a large shopping bag. "I'm going to make you a memory quilt with these shirts."

I still have that quilt and I can honestly say that if there were a fire in my home, this would be the first thing I would take with me.

In most cases, sorting though and clearing out your husband's clothes and other possessions will not have to be done immediately. You are in the midst of an emotional marathon and going through everything can bring up painful memories. I took my time to sort through things. Roy's personal objects, as small and trivial as they might have been, could bring me to tears in an instant, and I am definitely not alone in that response. However, the process is different for everyone. Some widows feel compelled to clear everything out right away, perhaps in an effort to gain control over the situation. This is one area where you should listen to your heart and not let anyone (including your relatives) pressure you into anything.

LUCKILY, A MONTH ONLY HAS THIRTY DAYS

The first month of this new phase in your life will be overwhelming. The best advice we can give is to be kind to yourself and take good care of you. We can assure you that you will survive, and the pain will become less intense. Angela, who has been a widow for five years, says, "I would tell any new widow that the emotional and physical pain you feel will not stay forever. The pain is something you have to work through. Depend on your family and friends for support, and if you don't have any, go find someone to talk with to help you move past the deep sadness and loss. Take time to talk with your children— every day if possible—about the parent they lost, even if this is painful at first. When you feel overwhelmed, just breathe and take your time to make decisions. You will slowly see little pieces of light, and those pieces of light are happiness and hope."

YEARS TWO TO FIVE AND BEYOND

How long does recovery take? You may well be asking yourself this question. And you may also be wondering: How long will I feel bad?

These are great questions, and we wish we had a great answer. The truth is that there is no set date after which you will feel better and will no longer be crying yourself to sleep or thinking about your spouse several times an hour on a certain date. Some mental health experts say that it usually takes a minimum of two years to make a successful recovery from any trauma or crisis.

We think this definitely holds true for widows. While many people—widows included—believe they will start feeling better within a few weeks, maybe a few months at most, typically it takes much longer. And it doesn't matter what your trauma or crisis was, whether it was major surgery, a physical assault, a divorce, or the death of someone close to you, it will take at least two years to begin to make a recovery and begin to transition to the next phase of your life. Many widows we interviewed for this book told us they were in their fourth, fifth, or even sixth year before they were starting to feel "normal" again. Kristin was in the sixth year of her journey toward successful coping when she approached Jim about writing this book.

In each of the first seven chapters of this book, we will remind you that recovery and transitioning takes time, and in those chapters, we will point out the challenges you may still encounter as you go past the second or third year. We can assure you that you will survive. It may simply take longer than you expected.

CHAPTER ONE TAKEAWAYS

- *It's normal to feel like you are in a fog for the first several days, weeks, or even months after your spouse dies.*
- *A Week Two To-Do list can help you sort out what you need to do ASAP.*
- *During Week Three, deal with medical bills, unneeded insurance policies, social media accounts, and phone calls.*
- *In Week Four, deal with tasks that should be done by the end of the first month.*
- *Consult our list of six ways to maintain your sanity during this stage of your life.*
- *You need help. Ask for it.*
- *Consider therapy, grief counseling, or a widow support group.*

Remember to read Chapter Nine, "Your Game Plan." It includes a customizable set of to-do lists where you can write down your personal tasks for this month. Or you can customize the same to-do lists online at KristinMeekhof.com, where you'll find all the Game Plan tools in this book.

chapter two

living on empty

coping with your feelings and getting support in the first years

MY HUSBAND DIED NOVEMBER 13, 2007. HERE'S WHAT I wrote in my journal on January 13, 2008:

> It has been two months today since my beloved husband died. I can't even write the words without crying. My world ended. I feel so lost, uncertain. There was no lonelier walk I ever took than when I went to Roy's grave on December 8 (his birthday was December 9) and walked in perfect snow to his grave to put an angel ornament on his graveside wreath. My beloved husband gone. I have avoided keeping a journal because the pain is too great, too raw.

I made another journal entry on February 3, less than a month later:

> My faith is still alive. I'm just very hurt, disappointed, disillusioned, raw, sad, depressed. Vacillating between despair because he's gone and gratitude that my husband did not suffer more. That we left nothing unsaid. That his last words to me were, "I love you."

When I started to write about my husband's death, I wasn't eager to take on the task. I am generally a very private person, and I was far more comfortable talking to other widows and writing about their loss. I wasn't sure I would be able to recapture the intense pain and emotion of my first year, or that I wanted to. Then I found these two lone entries, the only ones in the journal. I had forgotten that I wrote them. In seconds, I was pulled back to the first few months of my widowhood. Like it or not, I remembered the details. I realized that if I could write about it then, I could do it now.

I had tucked this journal away in a box of items from that painful, black time in my life. The contents of that box were like souvenirs from a trip I didn't want to remember: a notepad with a grocery list Roy had written, a check he'd signed but never sent, a stone he had found on our trip to Acadia National Park, a sticky note on which he had written a good friend's name and phone number. All these trinkets from our life together were on his desk when the hospital bed was delivered to our home. We had to rearrange his office to make space for the large bed. I had swept the scraps of paper and little mementos off his desktop and into the box, so we could move the desk against a wall. I hadn't looked inside the box until we started writing this book. That's when I read my two brief journal entries.

I think back to when I wrote those entries, once again feeling the aching pain and loneliness. We had no children together, so after work, I came home to complete silence. There was nothing to distract me. To make matters worse, the months following Roy's death were in the midst of a Michigan winter. This meant it was dark by 6 p.m., and cold. Curled up with a blanket on the couch, I fantasized that I would quit my job as a social worker, move to Hawaii, and walk on the beach. It was just a fantasy, of course. The reality was that I needed a job and health insurance. In the weeks between January 13 and February 3, I began to feel like maybe I had moved a few small degrees out of my initial shock and grief. But I know now I was still in the initial phases. For most people who lose a spouse, it takes a long time for grief to start to resolve itself. When it does, though, it is in tiny, barely noticeable degrees.

After interviewing more than one hundred widows, I can say for certain that there is no person, therapy, cruise, or prayer that will delete the pain and emotional suffering you experience after losing a spouse. Yes, work, reading, exercise, dinner out with friends—all of these activities provide a distraction. Children require your love and attention. But eventually, you have no choice. You have to face the loneliness. As the saying goes, "The only way out is through."

It doesn't matter how your spouse died or how loving the relationship was at the time of his death. The fact is that you will feel emotions you have never felt before, some of them quite unexpected. Many recently widowed women we interviewed asked what they could do to ease the raw sadness they were experiencing. All we could say was that if we knew the answer to that, we would be the first to share it. But there is no magic elixir for the situation in which you find yourself. You have endured one of life's worst traumas, and now comes the survival part. It begins with learning about the emotions you're experiencing now and those that may come later.

Letting go of the life you lived is scary. Getting support is crucial to dealing with your feelings and functioning in your everyday life. The support we encourage you to seek and the suggestions we offer throughout this book will come much more easily if you know what to expect emotionally. In addition, knowing what to expect will reassure you that you're not going crazy and have not fallen into a pit of despair from which you will never climb out. These emotions will evolve and fade—it's all part of the grieving process. But the feelings can be intense, and they can feel permanent, and that can be danger-ous if you are in a position where you must make decisions that will affect your future.

The standard warning to widows is, "Don't change anything for one year." That's excellent advice, if you have the option. But many widows don't. They must make choices about money, work, housing, and much more. Your best defense against making unwise decisions is to be aware of when your feelings may be distorting your judgment, and know when to ask the opinion of someone with a clearer head.

In this chapter, we'll look at the difficult emotions you are likely to face in the first months and years, and then we'll talk about the types of support that are available to you.

TWO CLICHÉS THAT ARE ACTUALLY TRUE

In the months to come, you will hear (and possibly say) two things time and again: "It's a roller coaster," and "Take one day at a time." When people told me to take one day at a time, it would annoy me (which is a normal reaction, by the way). Of course I was going to take one day at a time—what other choice did I have? But after a while I was comforted by that thought.

Christine Cantrell, PhD, a clinical psychologist in Royal Oak, Michigan, with an extensive background in the fields of pastoral ministry and grief counseling, says, "You don't just go through the five steps as outlined by Kübler-Ross,[1] and then you're done. Instead, you go over and over the steps. Sometimes you get stuck in a step for a while. Or one day you hear a song on the radio and it becomes a cue that causes sadness. It sets you off. It is definitely a roller-coaster ride."

Dr. Cantrell, who was a grief counselor with hospice and has worked with widows for more than twenty years, points out that it was once thought that people recovered from a loss within half a year. "We used to say six months, but that doesn't really hold up. When I work with people I don't have a time frame."

Cantrell suggests there are many factors that are relatively unique for each individual. "People who had hospice come in and work with them prior to their husband's death are generally better

---

1. Dr. Cantrell is referring to the five steps of grief as postulated by Elisabeth Kübler-Ross in the 1960s: denial, anger, bargaining, depression, acceptance. It's important to note that these steps are not intended as a gauge for recovery. And while you may experience some (or all) of them, they may not be in the order originally given by Kübler-Ross. You also may experience none of them.

prepared. And it helps if they have a support system—that can make a big difference."

Cantrell notes that some people feel numb the first year, and after that they start to feel the pain. "But grief often continues well beyond that first year because the loss is always there." That, she adds, is where the old adage about taking one day at a time comes in.

THE EMOTIONS OF BEREAVEMENT

About five years after my husband died, I read the beautiful memoir *A Widow's Story* by Joyce Carol Oates. She brilliantly captures those awkward and painful days following her husband's funeral. Tired of answering others' questions about how she is feeling, she writes, "I am thinking of having a T-shirt printed:

YES MY HUSBAND DIED.
YES I AM VERY SAD.

YES YOU ARE KIND TO OFFER CONDOLENCES.
NOW CAN WE CHANGE THE SUBJECT?"

I can relate. You know that yellow packing tape that has the word *Fragile* printed on it? I felt as if someone had stuck that tape all over my body. Following Roy's death, conversations were painfully awkward. People would not know what to say, and I thought they expected me to burst into tears at any moment. Certainly there were times when I felt fragile, but it wasn't twenty-four hours a day, as they seemed to assume. I longed for a normal conversation so I could focus on something else, even if it was only for fifteen minutes. I became the artful dodger, only talking with a handful of close confidants. What I don't think others understood is that it was stressful when they launched into carefully phrased, impromptu therapy sessions.

I remember meeting a friend for coffee. As she walked into the coffeehouse, I could see that she was upset. Her face was filled with tension. Right away, I asked what was wrong. She said, "I feel funny even telling you this because I know that you've been through so much worse, but I'm having a bad day."

I reassured her that it was fine and that I would like to know what happened. "I'm running late because when I went to drop Kevin off at preschool, another child walked over to me and I thought he was going to give me a hug. Instead he threw up on me. His mother didn't even apologize, and she saw the whole thing!"

I almost choked with laughter and then caught myself. I suddenly realized that I hadn't laughed like that in what seemed like weeks. Small moments like these reassured me that I still knew how to laugh. That meant that deep down, I was still myself. Grief is an emotional marathon, but these moments bring relief to the days when you're so sad and lost that you barely recognize yourself.

Who am I now? Many widows told us that this question occurred to them in the first weeks and months after their spouses' deaths. While it's true that you are much more than just a widow, it's also true that you will experience things differently as a widow. In addition to the feelings you may expect, like sadness and loneliness, you may be swamped by other emotions and sensations that are totally unfamiliar— pessimism, listlessness, an inability to focus, lack of motivation, loss of identity, disorientation. You don't feel like your old self, and you don't know how you will fit into the future.

Some widows report that they feel like aliens. What used to be boring, everyday life now seems like a golden, unattainable dream. You can remember that charmed world and see others living in it, but you are (temporarily!) cut off from it. You find you can't laugh at things you used to find hilarious. You may not feel sympathetic toward friends who are going through minor issues because your loss dwarfs their trivial worries or stresses. You may not even be able to get angry or excited by something that would have infuriated or elated you before. This is totally normal.

Scenes from your loss may keep playing over and over in your mind as well. This is also normal. For some, however, this relentless mental replay is similar to post-traumatic stress disorder (PTSD). They have nightmares or paralyzing flashbacks. It's not uncommon, but if you are experiencing this and it doesn't fade after two or three months, you should definitely seek professional help.

We don't mean to imply that the only emotions you will feel from now on will be negative. As we mentioned earlier, new widows can still laugh and be distracted by movies or music or meals with friends. As time passes, you will regain your inner balance and your personality will reemerge. This death will change you, but eventually you will feel like your old self again. The core you *is* still there.

When talking about the emotions of bereavement, Elisabeth Kübler-Ross's five stages of grief sometimes come up. These stages are denial, anger, bargaining, depression, and acceptance. The five stages don't really reflect what most widows experience; our understanding of the grieving process has evolved since Kübler-Ross introduced the concept in 1969. Psychologist Will Meek, writing in *Psychology Today* in 2012, explains:

> One of the key things most people don't know about those original five stages is that Kübler-Ross was writing about people *confronting their own death*, not the death of a loved one. Several groups of counselors later took the idea and used it to help people understand the loss of someone else. However, almost no scientific research has shown the existence of those stages, or that people go through stages at all.
>
> Over the past fifteen years or so, a much richer body of work has revealed a variety of different understandings and conclusions. The most important of these is that grief is (a) a highly individualized process, (b) has no specific timetable, and (c) many people find that their lives are *better* after going through grief, due to something referred to as "post-stress growth."

Richard Tedeschi, a psychologist at the University of North Carolina at Charlotte, along with fellow UNCC psychologist,

Lawrence Calhoun, started a research project a few years ago by interviewing survivors of severe injuries. They then went on to survey older people who had lost their spouses. They found that person after person told them the same thing: they wished deeply that they had not lost a spouse or been paralyzed, but nonetheless, the experience changed them for the better.

Tedeschi and Calhoun began to see patterns in trauma survivors. People reported positive change in five areas: they had a renewed appreciation for life, they found new possibilities for themselves, they felt more personal strength, their relationships improved, and they felt spiritually more satisfied. In 1995, Tedeschi and Calhoun coined a term for what they were finding: "posttraumatic growth." Out of trauma and the personal tragedy of losing a beloved spouse, you can experience remarkable growth.

As Tedeschi and Calhoun, along with a number of other researchers and clinicians, have discovered, it is normal to have problems following trauma. You could lose sleep, have terrible images replay in your head, be racked by guilt or fear. No matter how you react to your trauma and loss, you will recover. Tedeschi and others say that the majority of people grow as a result of their suffering. Paradoxically, many grow even as they suffer. The way we cope with trauma is far more complex than once thought, and the way it molds us is similarly complex. "We bend, we break, we repair and rebuild, and often we grow, changing for the better in ways we never would have if we had not suffered" is the way Jim Rendon, a New York writer, puts it.

Many of us eventually move from intense suffering into something referred to as "integrated grief," which is when we have a backdrop of bittersweet memories that can occasionally emerge for many years into the future, but do not overwhelm us when they do. Once they reach this place, many people say they have a better outlook on life, live more intentionally, and rearrange their priorities. A growing number of therapists (including us) see this as one of the desirable end points of the grieving process.

These are important ideas to remember as you travel this road you never wanted to be on. As impossible as it may seem right now, the pain will not last forever—and you can't predict how you, personally, will handle it. That being said, most people can expect some powerful and difficult emotions during the first year of widowhood. Keep in mind that this is not a definitive list—your own feelings may be far more varied and subtle.

Fear

One of the first emotions a new widow is likely to experience is fear. It may be a sense of panic or a pervasive dread. The fear is fueled by thoughts like, "How can I make it without my husband by my side?" and, "He's always taken care of me; I won't be able to function without him!" For almost every widow, the fear is related to suddenly being alone and having to make decisions without a loving partner by her side. One widow recalled, "After my husband died, I realized that our marriage had been like a magic carpet that was always underneath me, holding me up in the air. It felt like that carpet had been yanked away and I had crashed down onto the sidewalk."

Here is what other widows said about their fears:

> ### WHAT WIDOWS SAID
>
> There was sadness and loss, yes, but even more was the feeling of being over my head. I would have to deal with things I had never dealt with before, like writing an obituary and deciding what I would say at a memorial service.
>
> —MARY, 57

I was petrified to go on without him. I felt left behind, exposed, and unprotected by the husband I thought was so powerful and invincible.

—SHARLEEN, 38

Certainly, there was fear. My biggest fear was, "how will I get through this financially?" I wasn't working and suddenly I was on my own.

—AUDREY, 49

When I thought about the remainder of my life, knowing that I was still relatively young and that I would most likely live decades without him, I was terrified.

—MINDY, 36

Anxiety

Having to face any new and unfamiliar situation will trigger anxiety in most of us. "A widow feels anxiety because the fabric of her world has been ripped apart," says psychologist Steven Ceresnie, PhD, who specializes in depression and grief work. "She is at first numb to the loss, and yearns for a return to a reality that never will be."

Anxiety is one of the most predictable emotions you will face after the loss of your husband. It will appear for most widows as nervousness, feeling shaky, and a general sense of unease. We have all experienced anxiety in its mild forms, when waiting for an important phone call or email, just before a critical test or exam, or going to the dentist. But in its more serious form—which could occur after losing a loved one—you might feel panic with a jittery sensation, sweating, obsessive thoughts, and even nightmares.

Weeks after Roy's death, my doctor noticed I had lost weight. I told her about my anxiety and how it was making me not want to eat. I was often anxious about things I couldn't even articulate. I also worried I was slipping into a state of depression. Looking back, I think I was experiencing generalized anxiety, which is a common emotion reported by the widows we interviewed. One widow even had a name for it. She called it "widow's brain." She said it meant that small tasks, like grocery shopping or driving a long distance alone, seem overwhelming. For me, it felt as if my brain had short-circuited. There were small things to do, but it felt as if it would take a great deal of effort to accomplish them. For a stranger looking at my day's agenda, things appeared normal; there was nothing funeral related or death related. But one incident not going as planned would send me into a panic.

WHAT WIDOWS SAID

For about six months, I had heart palpitations. Sometimes it felt like I was having a heart attack and other times like my heart would beat out of my chest. I soon learned it was anxiety and if I just relaxed and tried to think of something else, the anxiety would go away. I think you just have to try to survive for the first few months and the pain will subside.

—JULIE, 34

At first after Meredith died, I was nervous and anxious all the time. I would be sitting and reading and find that my legs were shaking or that I had a queasy feeling in my stomach. I had nightmares every night. And then I would think about those dreams during the day and that would make me even more anxious. I guess you could say I was a real mess for a long time.

—PENNY, 47

I had health problems in the two years after Franklin died.

I think it was probably the stress and worry after his death that caused me to have physical problems. Maybe I wasn't watching what I was eating and I probably wasn't taking care of myself. After he died, I had the pressure of dealing by myself with our handicapped son.

—BRENDA, 56

I did a lot of worrying after my husband died of cancer when we were both thirty-one. I had two children and I worried about the future. Could I raise the kids alone? How was I going to support them? It just left me fatigued and anxious. I'm happy to say that that passed in time.

—CARRIE, 35

Shock and Disorientation

Shock is an almost inevitable reaction when your spouse dies. We found this to be true even among women who knew their partners were terminally ill. It is as if we don't believe that someone we love will really die. When they do, the response is, "How could this happen?"

In my case, I knew Roy had advanced adrenal cancer and there was no cure for it. We had talked about him dying, but when he actually passed away, I was stunned. It had only been eight weeks since we had first gone to the doctor, assuming he had bronchitis. I remember thinking, "This can't have happened to me! He was just walking on the treadmill beside me three weeks ago. He passed the stress test at the hospital. We couldn't even get a handicapped parking sticker because the primary care doctor said he could walk just fine. He can't be dead—not yet!"

The line can be blurry between the initial, intense shock and the disorientation that can last for weeks or months. One Saturday afternoon a few weeks after Roy died, I felt particularly exhausted and decided to take a nap. I set my alarm and woke up a few hours later. I thought, "Something feels odd," so I got up, walked to my front door, and found that it was ajar. My keys were still in the lock, and I had propped open the storm door so I could carry some groceries in. Shaking my head in disbelief, I removed the keys and shut the storm door. I went to the kitchen to find the freezer door open and a tub of ice cream melted on the counter. I had no recollection of bringing the groceries inside.

One widow said that for the first six weeks, "I felt like I was walking around in a haze." Other women we interviewed had similar reactions:

WHAT WIDOWS SAID

My husband became abusive and threatening and my lawyer had him removed from the house after I filed for a divorce. In order to keep the house, I had to give him $90,000... The check arrived to give to him, but that same day I got a telephone call late in the afternoon... The officer told me that they had found my husband dead in his apartment. They figured he had been dead for a few days. That was when the ground opened up under me. I had never been physically shaken before like that and hope to never feel this way again.

—YOLANDA, 48

I felt completely in shock. It was difficult to absorb what had happened. The funeral and the early weeks after my husband's death felt unreal, like a dream I would wake up from. I felt very ineffectual, like I was trying to walk through peanut butter and couldn't get where I needed to go. Time got strange. Some days seemed to go on forever. Others flew by and I couldn't figure out what I had been doing while they passed—I got up, showered, sat drinking coffee looking at the bird feeder, and then...the day was over? What was I doing while it went by? I couldn't focus.. I usually love to read, and many friends gave me gifts of long novels to distract me, but I couldn't even finish a newspaper article. When I look back on that time now, I hardly remember it. There are things I took care of that I don't remember taking care of, people who say they visited and I have no memory of the visit. It's strange, because I have a vivid, crystal-clear memory of many details from the week Jim was dying that I would like to forget. Those memories from right before his death are burned into my brain. But after? I was a zombie for a while.

—MARLENE, 51

I was still living in a fog. This was true even before he died because I knew he was ill, but I didn't know what was wrong. That was the thing that caused me to be in a fog—I didn't know what he was suffering from.

—PHYLLIS, 48

There's a lack of focus in my life. I feel like I have adult ADD. I find myself being disorganized about getting things done. I stand, say, in the kitchen, looking out the window, and I daydream... Suddenly an hour or two has gone by. It is like I have had a seizure. It's a strange sensation of time. It seems to slow down and then at other times it speeds up. I have a lot of trouble planning things. I was a big planner before; now I'm afraid to plan anything. The day of the funeral, we were supposed to be in Paris for my birthday. If I need to plan anything, I don't bother, because I think it will go wrong.

—SONYA, 48

Loneliness

Of all the emotions widows described, none was mentioned as often as loneliness. Joanna, 55, told us, "I expected sadness and anger, but I didn't know I would feel this incredible feeling of loneliness." Joanna's husband died of a rare blood disorder, a condition that came on suddenly. She went on to say: "Since he died, I've been going on a lot of trips, spending time with friends and relatives. Coming back from trips, on a train or an airplane, I look at the person next to me and think, "Why am I sitting next to a stranger? My husband is supposed to be next to me." At night I often cry myself to sleep. During the day, I think he could be at work or at a conference…he'll be home soon."

Another widow, Dodie, 56, concurred: "Everything reminds me of him, every day. I'm told it will get easier. The loneliness resulting from the loss of his love and companionship is devastating. I see people for lunch or ice skating, but then I have to come home. My son and his wife come to see me and help with tasks. And then they go home. I go to visit my daughter in Chicago, but then I come home. The truth is what Edna St. Vincent Millay wrote: 'Where you used to be, there is a hole in the world, which I find myself constantly walking around in the daytime, and falling into at night.'"

Sadness and Depression

The overriding emotions for all the widows interviewed were sadness and depression. When you are depressed, it interferes with your daily life and makes it difficult to perform even basic tasks. Depressive disorders can take several forms, and you should be aware of which form you are experiencing.

- ❧ *Clinical depression* (also called a *major depressive disorder*) is characterized by several symptoms that interfere with your ability to work, sleep, study, eat, or enjoy once-pleasurable activities. Clinical depression is disabling and will continually prevent you from functioning normally.
- ❧ *Chronic depression* (also called a *dysthymic disorder*) is a mild but

long-term form of depression that persists for two years or longer, with symptoms that may not be severe enough to disable you but may well prevent you from functioning at your normal capacity or from feeling like your old self.

✳ *Situational depression* is a short-term form of depression that can occur in the aftermath of various traumatic events in your life, including the loss of a spouse. Psychologists sometimes refer to this condition as an adjustment disorder. Your symptoms may be more or less identical to those of someone with clinical depression with certain key differences. One difference is that given time, situational depression will go away.

✳ *A minor depression*, which you will without a doubt experience in the beginning, is a depressive episode lasting at least two weeks. It will not be so disabling that it could be called a major depression. However, as Dr. Cantrell observes, "Depression does set in; certainly that is common. But it's all part of a natural process, and you need the natural process to proceed to heal. A widow must allow herself to follow along with this natural process. Some people fight it by, for instance, not allowing themselves to cry. But crying can be healthy— emotionally and physically."

SYMPTOMS OF DEPRESSION

- Persistent sad, anxious, or empty feelings
- Feelings of hopelessness or pessimism
- Feelings of guilt, worthlessness, or helplessness
- Irritability, restlessness
- Loss of interest in once-pleasurable activities or hobbies
- Fatigue and decreased energy
- Difficulty concentrating, remembering details, and making decisions

- Insomnia, early-morning wakefulness, or excessive sleeping
- Overeating or loss of appetite
- Thoughts of suicide, suicide attempts
- Aches or pains, headaches, cramps, or digestive problems that do not ease even with treatment

Obviously, you are expected to feel sadness when you sustain a major loss. Time is a great healer, and eventually you will recover and be able to function like your normal self again. However, if your depression doesn't begin to ease after a few weeks, and if it is accompanied by frequent crying, feelings of hopelessness, withdrawal, thoughts of suicide, and an inability to resume a normal life, you should talk to a professional about your emotions. If you have been contemplating ending your own life, you need to seek a doctor's help immediately. You may feel overwhelmed right now, but suicide is not the answer.

Many widows with a depressive illness never seek treatment. But the majority, even those with the most severe depression, can improve with the support of a mental health professional. Medication, psychotherapy, and other recognized treatments can help you overcome chronic or clinical depression.

WHAT WIDOWS SAID

I had this overwhelming grief. In my family, when I was growing up, no one was allowed to feel sad. Because of this I didn't feel comfortable, but I know I felt sadness. For one thing, I felt sad that this had to happen to him.

—ELAINE, 66

Jim died from a heart attack on the second day of our family vacation at the beach. I felt pain and sadness for months. But I would tell other widows that the emotional pain you feel will not stay forever. As my life has begun to open up in new ways, my pain has started to recede.

—JACKIE, 45

Anger

One thing we discovered as we talked to widows was how seldom they said they felt anger. Kübler-Ross's second stage of grief is anger, and many of us believed that this was an essential part of the grieving process. But very few of the women we talked to said they felt angry. For those that did reveal they felt angry toward their spouse or the situation, it wasn't always specifically for dying.

For example, Pam, 56, said she was pissed at her husband when he was ill prior to his death for "pretending to be sicker than he was; at least that was what I thought at the time. I see now that I didn't understand his illness any more than the doctors did." Another widow said she would get angry with her husband for talking about dying: "I was mad because I thought that would make it easier for him to die."

Sydney, 37, expressed her anger in a particularly articulate way:

I felt angry, but I wasn't sure who I was angry at. The medical team gave it their best shot. Our family worked together well. There was no person to be angry at. My daughter said she wanted to "punch God in the face." But I don't believe God causes suffering. So I was just angry that my husband died rather than feeling angry at anyone or anything. It felt unfair. He was a good person, a good father, a professor, and a psychotherapist who gave a lot to a lot of people. He led a healthy lifestyle; he followed medical advice. He did all the right things and he still died. I was angry that I didn't get more time with him, angry that my life didn't turn out how I had expected it to, angry that my children had to lose their father and won't get to have him at their graduations and weddings. I get angry when I see couples arguing and I picture myself lecturing them, telling them how lucky they are and that they should appreciate each other more. I feel angry when I see an elderly couple holding hands, because I won't get to have that. I don't want to take it away from them. I just want it for myself too.

Rita's husband died twenty-six years ago, when she was fifty-one and he was fifty-three. They had four children who were in college at the time. She recalls: "The most difficult thing to deal with was the constant feeling of unfairness. He wasn't going to be here and we couldn't enjoy him… I kept in this anger, this feeling of unfairness. It wasn't fair to him or to me. I've never gotten over it."

Yet sometimes there was no anger where you might expect it. Krissy's husband took his life; his mother had also committed suicide. He had been laid off at age fifty-nine and slipped into a depression. "I wasn't angry at him," Krissy said. "I felt love and compassion. I knew how troubled he must have been, and then with his mother's death. I can't imagine what he was going through… His kids were angry. They would express anger in front of me—not at me, just anger that he would do that… A lot of people told me I should get angry, but I couldn't. It just wasn't me. I didn't feel anger."

Guilt

A great many widows are plagued by guilt. A common source of guilt is the feeling that you could have done more.

I know I felt guilty after Roy died. He had seemed so normal, even healthy. We had received the diagnosis that he had adrenal cancer, and we knew no treatment was going to prevent him from dying. But when he was gone, I had doubts about what I should have or could have done: *I should have recognized that he was sick. I should have known something was wrong. If I had recognized the symptoms early enough, maybe his life could have been saved.* The guilt stayed with me until I went back to the Cancer Center at the University of Michigan Hospital and talked to their renowned adrenal cancer specialist, Dr. Gary Hammer. I voiced my guilt to him.

"Kristin," he said, "you did everything you could have done."

It was such a relief to hear those words. I no longer had to carry around that burden, along with everything else I was trying to deal with after Roy's death.

A widow's guilt usually comes in the form of self-doubt, regret, or self-recrimination. Maybe there is something you think you could have done to spare his life or something you didn't do that would have eased his dying. Maybe there was something you said or failed to say that you cannot undo. Guilt can stick around for years, but like the other responses to loss, it often fades with time.

When we asked Dr. Christine Cantrell about the guilt widows may feel, she said that whether or not they feel guilt often depends on the reason for the death. "If it was a car accident that they were both in and only the husband died, there may be survivor's guilt." However, Cantrell said that guilt is less common when the death was expected. She added, "In hospice, we tried to have people say things to each other that needed to be said. They can help eliminate the need to feel guilty." Guilt and loyalty often lead widows to refrain from dating. "They may feel like dating is being disloyal," Cantrell says. "They may make a vow that they will never laugh again or never date. In hospice, we try to get the husband to give permission to his wife to date after his death, so there is no sense of being disloyal or guilty."

WHAT WIDOWS SAID

I was feeling guilty that I hadn't gotten into bed with him at the nursing home. And that I hadn't thought of breaking him out of the nursing home and bringing him home so he could have died in the home he loved.

—ELAINE, 66

I'm not much of a drinker, so I had a hard time understanding his alcoholism. I felt so guilty after he died. I should have tried to do more to help him with his drinking. I should have tried harder to get him help. I finally came to the realization that I did what I could do to help him—the rest was up to him.

—MARILYN, 51

I weirdly felt guilty that he died instead of me. He was funnier, a better storyteller, one of those larger-than-life characters who seemed to deserve to be alive more than I did. For a long time I would feel guilty that I was alive to see beautiful things, like fall leaves, and he wasn't.

—RHONDA, 47

He died twenty days before our divorce was final. To add to my guilt, my husband had not changed the beneficiary of his life insurance nor of his 401(k). I received both. They didn't add up to a fortune, and I split the insurance with my children and paid off their student loans, but I felt guilty that we were going to be divorced and I got his insurance and his retirement account.

—CLARISSA, 61

Once the shock wore off, guilt and grieving settled in. Some nights I would howl crying, scaring both the dog and myself. I went into therapy to try to deal with the guilt. I had thrown him out and in a sense I was responsible for his dying alone, slowly suffocating from congestive heart failure. Had I not thrown him out, I would have seen the sickness and forced him into treatment. It was my fault—all my fault. I still feel it today, just not as severely.

—ANITA, 56

Loss of Identity

What strikes nearly every widow is that after years of being a wife, she is suddenly single again, only it's a very sad version of single. The word "widow" brings to mind shapeless black dresses, deprivation, and lifelong mourning. No one wants to be a widow. What's more, you don't have any training for it. You do not see yourself as single or widow. In the case of a sudden death, one minute you're going along fine as a wife, and the next you have that role ripped away from you. If you have children, you go from being part of a nuclear family to being a single mom.

Any time you lose the comfort of one role and are forced into another, the result is anxiety, stress, and feeling at loose ends. You may find yourself panicking: "What am I supposed to do now? How do I do this?" It will take time to learn this new role. Experts say most people should give themselves a good two years to recover from an emotional trauma such as the loss of a beloved spouse. If your husband died unexpectedly, it could take longer.

Once you get used to the idea that grieving is going to be a long process, you can relax and accept that for the time being you are not all right. You experienced a major trauma, and you need time to recover. Some widows said it was five or six years before they began to feel whole again. It's worth mentioning, too, that many widows are remarried or in long-term relationships within a few years of a spouse's death. By that time, they have integrated the loss, largely come to terms with it, and have become comfortable in their new roles.

Here is how some widows described their loss of identity upon losing their spouse:

WHAT WIDOWS SAID

I was no longer a caretaker. After my husband died, I wandered around the house thinking, "What am I supposed to do?" This was despite the fact that I worked full-time in an office. But I was so used to spending all of my time outside of work caring for him.

—NOREEN, 49

When my husband was diagnosed with the disease that led to his death, he had just taken a new job and we had just moved to a different city. I had given up my job and my community, and our children were in college and graduate school. My plan had been to fix up the new house and explore the new city while my husband settled into his new job. Then suddenly my job became 24-7 caretaker. After he died, when I came back to the house, I felt like I had lost all my identities in one fell swoop—wife, mother, psychotherapist, longtime member of a community. I felt invisible, like there was no place for me in the world. I thought about moving back to the city we had lived in for thirty years, but that place was so full of memories, and it was a place I had lived in as a wife and mother. This identity issue has been the hardest thing I have dealt with, and I am still actively dealing with it.

—SUZANNE, 54

I was very proud of who he was and what he did. And I felt a part of it. The sense of loss I felt was similar to losing a limb. A part of you is lost and you'll never get it back and, therefore, you are not the same person you were. For me, the me I was, was no longer complete.

—IRENE, 72

The fact that I was now a single mother really bothered me. I'll admit I had always felt proud about the fact that my husband and I had stayed together through some hard times because we really loved each other and being parents was so important to us. Now I'd have to do it all by myself—like the divorced moms I used to see after school, picking up their kids, looking stressed out.

—ANGIE, 42

I really loved being a wife to Roy. I didn't feel like I was in a captive, limited relationship. I loved being there for him, living with him, and feeling like we were traveling together in this journey called life. When he died, that role or identity of wife also ended. It took me months to fully realize how much I missed not only him, but being a wife. I attempted to fill the void with other things, like running and doing advocacy for cancer-related organizations, and that did help, but naturally it could not replace the married life I had treasured.

The emotions we have talked about may not be the complete list of feelings you will experience, but they are the most common emotions widows have shared with us. While you will face many other challenges, coping with your emotions is the most difficult one, especially the first year. We hope you will find some comfort in the knowledge that these emotions are normal and transitory. We do not believe that there is really such a thing as closure over the loss of a spouse, but we have seen that the great majority of widows transition out of grief and into the rest of their lives, in which they function normally. As surreal and insurmountable as early grief might feel, it is a path that every human being must travel at some time.

MANAGING YOUR EMOTIONS: BYRON KATIE'S TURNAROUNDS

Whatever feelings you encounter in the first several months, one of the toughest aspects of grief is that you are alone with it. If you have children, you can't constantly talk with them about the loss of their dad. Even if your therapist has encouraged you not to hide your feelings from your kids, common sense tells you not to share all your adult-sized anguish with them. No one has enough friends and family members to absorb all the pain, so you may need to find reliable ways to discharge some of it. Some widows join a support group or enter into therapy (we'll talk more about that a little later). Others find that exercise—yoga, running, biking, hiking—is a good way to relieve stress. True, these are only distractions, but any one of them is healthier than sitting and ruminating about your loss and sorrow.

Sometimes our biggest enemy is our own mind. We can set ourselves up for failure and more loneliness. It goes something like this: "I know I shouldn't be disappointed if I don't get invited to that party, but I really want to go. Should I say something? No, I don't want to appear needy. Well, I am needy—my husband just died. Why can't anyone understand how lonely I am?"

As a recent widow, you may be fatigued, you may be mostly eating whatever is put in front of you, and you may feel emotionally exhausted. Because of that, your thought patterns may be cyclical and illogical. "All the stress that we feel is caused by arguing with what is," says Byron Katie in her book *Loving What Is*. She recommends a four-step process to examine how our thoughts create stress, and then turning them around. This process is explained in her book and on her website (www.thework.com), and it can be used for all types of conflicts (work problems, addictions, relationships, and difficult emotions such as depression).

In its most basic form, Katie's "The Work," as she calls it, consists of four questions and turnarounds. First, you state the situation or fear that is causing you stress. For example, if you are having problems with your husband's children, your statement might be: "His son and daughter hate me and don't want me to be part of the family anymore." Then you ask yourself four questions:

1. Is it true? (Yes or no. If no, move to 3.)
2. Can you absolutely know that it's true? (Yes or no.)
3. How do you react—what happens—when you believe that thought?
4. Who would you be without the thought?

Here is how this process might unfold:

1. Is it true that his children hate me and want to exclude me from the family? (If you answer yes, go to the second question. If you answer no, move to the third question.)
2. Do I absolutely know that it's true? (Answer yes or no.) Continuing this example, you might think, "His daughter failed to invite me to a memorial service she held for her father, and his son wrote me a note saying that I wasn't their mother and they didn't have to include me in family celebrations."
3. How do I react—what happens—when I believe this thought? "It makes me sad and I feel unloved. I think too much about how I want to be part of his children's lives."
4. Who would I be without the thought? "I could spend more time and energy thinking about obtaining other support I need and other people who do want me in their lives."

The next steps have to do with what Katie calls "turnarounds." These are opportunities to experience the opposite of what you originally believed. A statement can be turned around to the self, to the other, and to the opposite (and sometimes to "my thinking," when that feels appropriate). The goal is to find at least three specific, genuine examples of how each turnaround is true in your life, and then allow yourself the time and presence to feel them deeply. This technique can help you accept your feelings, rather than deny them. Furthermore, by allowing yourself to think about your feelings, you can more effectively answer the last question.

For example, "His kids hate me" turns around to "I hate me." You would then try to find at least three specific, genuine examples of times you have hated yourself. You could also find turnarounds for thinking they do not want you to be part of the family. Your turnarounds could be: "I do not want to be part of the family." Or, "They really do want me to be part of the family." Or, "I don't need to be part of the family." In each instance, the goal is to find examples that support the turnaround. For instance: "They asked me to join them for the birthday dinner recently." Or, "When they asked me to join them for the dinner party, I made an excuse not to go." Or, "Instead of ruminating about not being invited to the party, I made arrangements to go out with other friends and I had a really good time."

You can also use turnarounds on your emotions. Let's take guilt. The statement that goes along with your guilt might be, "I feel guilty because I should have known he had a fatal disease and made sure he got help in time." The four questions you would ask yourself are:

1. Is it true that I should have known about his disease earlier? (If you answer yes, go to the second question. If you answer no, move to the third question).
2. Do I absolutely know that it's true that I should have known about his disease earlier? (Answer yes or no).
3. How do I react—what happens—when I believe this thought?
4. Who would I be without this thought?

In this example, the first question may require some research or confirmation from a doctor. When I consulted Dr. Hammer, he told me there was no way I could have known. And if I had known, there was nothing I could have done to prevent Roy from dying. So question two becomes a moot point. I would answer question three by saying that when I believe this thought, I end up beating myself up. And question four is an important one: Who would I be without this thought? I can answer that by thinking about what I have started to do with my life since I stopped being overwhelmed by guilt. I have begun writing and sharing my story with others; I have written this book to help other widows; I have become involved in raising awareness of adrenal cancer; I have become a person who tries to help other widows cope with their experiences.

While we can't guarantee that this technique will work for you and your troublesome emotions and conflicts, Byron Katie's work offers a solid alternate perspective for managing your feelings and relationships.

NAVIGATING DAILY LIFE

"Grief, when it comes, is nothing we expect it to be... Grief is different. Grief has no distance. Grief comes in waves, paroxysms, sudden apprehensions that weaken the knees and blind the eyes and obliterate the dailiness of life." Joan Didion wrote this after the death of her husband, in her poignant memoir *The Year of Magical Thinking*.

As Didion found out, grief changes everything. The normal trip to the grocery store triggers an emotional meltdown. You become a puddle when you see a letter addressed to your partner. The third installment to the movie trilogy you planned to see together is released, and watching a commercial for it sends you into a two-day slump.

As a widow, you may feel that you deserve a pass and that others should accept and excuse your meltdowns, your complaining, or your pessimism about the future. One young widow took it literally whenever someone asked, "How are you?"

Rebecca, 35, told us: "I find myself telling people in detail how my life is so miserable now that I'm a widow. I realize nobody wants to hear about how awful my life is without a husband. They will soon stop asking how I am and they will avoid seeing me altogether."

If you are a complainer or are so angry or depressed that you can't stop talking about your misery, your friends and relatives may avoid you. No longer will you be invited to the birthday parties or family events, and the phone will ring less often. Is it fair? Not really, but then again, these people have their own lives and concerns that you can't expect them to set aside just because your situation is worse right now. And fair or not, it is human nature to back away from people who are relentlessly depressed and depressing.

This doesn't mean you must suppress all your feelings. It means that to maintain your mental health, reduce further anxiety, and sustain relationships with others, you need to learn how to cope appropriately. You may be at the point where you are starting to process your emotions and not constantly thinking about them. But if your feelings are still new and raw, you have plenty of options.

- Join a support group
- Go to some private therapy sessions
- Talk to friends or relatives
- Find a religious community
- Exercise
- Keep a journal
- Cultivate diversions

JOIN A SUPPORT GROUP

Dr. Christine Cantrell told us she doubts that every widow needs to see a private therapist. She says that family support is huge and support from friends can be especially valuable. In addition, support groups may serve as an important bridge over this troubled passage.

Funeral homes may offer support groups, as do churches and counseling agencies. Some widows attend just one or a few sessions; others go for years. There's no right or wrong way to use a support group; they are simply an opportunity to be around people who understand what you are feeling.

Support groups for widows and widowers are easy to find in most towns and cities. You can google "bereavement groups" and your zip code, or you can contact a local mental health clinic or social service agency. If you belong to a house of worship, they will probably be able to point you to a group they run or are affiliated with. If you have not recently practiced a religion but are open to it now, most congregations will welcome you.

Support groups work very well for some widows but miss the mark for others:

WHAT WIDOWS SAID

I was twenty-nine when my husband died, and I was an elementary school teacher. We had no children. I tried various support groups but found that they weren't too helpful because I was so much younger. However, I met another young widow and this helped. Just getting together regularly to talk was therapeutic.

—FRANCES, 34

I called the Jewish Board of Family Services to find a support group about two months after my husband died. I was the youngest person in my group, and it was very comforting. I went for about six or eight months, and the group ended; otherwise I would have kept going.

—NANCY, 42

As my own social network of close friends and family members, such as my sister, drifted away from me, I looked beyond my immediate surroundings and slowly built a

> framework of support with other widows. No one else knows
> how to deal with a widow. Some treat you like you have the
> plague; some just don't know what to say. And to some you
> are a reminder of what could happen to them. Only widows
> get it. It's a crappy club, but I was a member, like it or not.
>
> —JILL, 46

GO TO PRIVATE THERAPY SESSIONS

Talking to an impartial third person who is trained in grief counseling usually helps to relieve sadness and depression. Although you shouldn't expect to be cured after a few sessions, it is comforting to know that once a week, for an hour, you can talk about anything without being judged. In a therapeutic relationship, you can share your present fears as well as your regrets.

Some widows like talking to a professional—a counselor, social worker, psychologist, or psychiatrist—because they don't want to burden relatives or friends or because a support group doesn't offer enough privacy. Other widows desire the full attention of a grief counselor, as opposed to having to listen to the stories of other widows and perhaps be made more depressed by them. Many therapists specialize in grief and loss, and there are organizations (such as state psychological associations) that can help you locate a therapist who is right for you.

If you don't immediately hit it off with the first therapist you try, go to one more session, address the issue, and then move on. One widow told us that her therapist looked like he was falling asleep. That wasn't okay, and she was right to seek another therapist. It is a vulnerable time for you, so you may not feel like confronting the therapist. If so, simply cancel your next session and look for a therapist who is a better fit.

Therapy was helpful for many of the widows we interviewed:

WHAT WIDOWS SAID

I went to approximately half a dozen therapy sessions. It helped me to sort out some of the family things that happened after the funeral. I needed a person to whom I could address questions and get some advice on how to handle sticky situations. This may not have relieved my grief, but it reduced some of my stress.

—BIANCA, 39

I didn't want to keep dumping everything on my friends, so I went to a therapist. She was very warm and friendly and helped me to face some feelings I had been avoiding. It was one of the best things I did that first year.

—AUBREY, 56

I did see a therapist, but it was a bit of a leap for me because I did traditional psychodynamically oriented talk therapy in my own practice, and had also been in that type of therapy several times in my life and found it enormously helpful. But I had this strong sense that what I was feeling went so deep that I couldn't touch it with words. So I met with a therapist who did sensorimotor therapy and EMDR [eye movement desensitization and reprocessing, an integrative psychotherapy approach that has been extensively researched and proven effective for the treatment of trauma], which focus on bodily sensations and emotion. I was a bit skeptical, but found it enormously helpful and freeing. Of course, I talked with the therapist quite a bit too, and one thing he did was help me realize how much time grief takes and how profound it is. I was being hard on myself because I felt

> others expected me to just be back in the saddle and do fine. They admired me for being strong and resilient, so I'd be disappointed in myself if I had a few bad days of crying and not being able to get things done. My therapist reinforced that I could be a strong and resilient person and still be grieving deeply, that that was okay, and that, in fact, being able to grieve is part of being resilient.
>
> —ASHLEY, 48

Going to see a therapist also means that you will likely be evaluated for a need for medication, such as antidepressants. Because of the intense unpleasant feelings many widows experience, medication can be quite helpful. In some instances, it is necessary:

WHAT WIDOWS SAID

> I didn't think he would die before me. So I was sad, and then it became depression. I actually started taking an antidepressant a few months before he died. Caring for him was just an unhappy time for me, watching him die. I started weaning myself off the antidepressant after he died. There are still times of depression, but nothing like when he first died. And I don't need to take antidepressants any longer.
>
> —DIANE, 54

> I felt such sadness, I couldn't move. I stayed in bed except to feed my dogs. My only job was to keep them and my plants alive. I couldn't have people around because when a wave of grief would come over me, my throat would fill

up with so much phlegm I'd have to stand over a sink or a toilet to throw up. This happened to me when I was in my car once, and I threw up spaghetti all over my lap. This went on for four months, until a good friend gently suggested I go on some sort of medication. I was afraid to do this. I felt that I needed to experience every moment of grief in order for it to be over. I went to a doctor and he prescribed a low dose of Prozac, and within a day the cloud lifted. I felt the burden of consistent sadness dissipate. And slowly I had me back—not the miserable stranger whom I couldn't recognize as myself.

—DONNA, 43

Joyce Carol Oates's memoir, *A Widow's Story*, includes a chapter called "The Cache." It begins with a list of thirteen medications, some over-the-counter and some prescription, that were in her cupboard. She writes, "The widow's drug cache, spread out on a counter, is a haphazard accumulation of years." She discusses the need to experience a deep sleep, "Otherwise, the widow is AWAKE. Never has there been such WAKEFULNESS through the interminable hours of the night sweaty, frankly scared—not as an adult but as a child is scared—trying not to think of the remainder of my life."

I mentioned earlier that a few weeks after Roy's death, my doctor noticed I had lost weight and I told her about my anxiety. I left the office that day with a prescription for Xanax and an antidepressant. Weeks later, I had side effects from the antidepressant: constant nausea and a chalky film in my mouth. The doctor put me on a different antidepressant, but the side effects persisted. I stopped taking the medications and found that I was functioning better without the medication. However, by that time, I was also exercising several days a week. When I increased my running and started going to yoga, my sleep improved. Like me, you may need psychiatric medication at first. But also like me, you may not like the side effects and you might find a more acceptable alternative.

TALK TO FRIENDS OR RELATIVES

Many of the widows we talked to had close relationships with their families and turned to them when they needed to talk about their troubled emotions. Girlfriends, too, were there to listen and provide a shoulder to cry on.

WHAT WIDOWS SAID

I had three girlfriends. They made me come to a meeting with them two times a week. For six months, I could cry or do whatever. I just had to meet with them. After about three years, I started getting my life together again. But they were my big support system.

—CAROLYN, 52

I am fortunate because I found what I call my "life savers." These are not necessarily people I knew before George died, although some are. Now they are my special people. The people I have surrounded myself with now, we can talk about my husband. It may be sad and make me cry at times, but I need to talk about him or have others talk about him. My life savers include some close girlfriends, but they also include my Zumba instructor, my personal trainer, and my hairdresser.

—DOREEN, 64

FIND A RELIGIOUS COMMUNITY

"A church or a synagogue is important because when you share emotional or religious beliefs and feelings, it brings you closer to people," Dr. Cantrell told us. "Being with a community that knew you and your husband is different from going to therapy, and it can be as helpful as therapy. A therapist never got to know your husband, but your friends within your religious community knew him and knew you together. This kind of support can be life-giving."

Going to church or another place of worship and talking to a minister, rabbi, or priest were very important for a large number of the women we interviewed:

WHAT WIDOWS SAID

It started at the hospital when our priest came to deliver last rites. But then he came to the house to be supportive. He talked to me about how I would tell our children that their father had died. He told me I was a strong woman and that really helped me because I didn't think of myself that way. Because of his support, I have been able to take all the skills I have and make good decisions and raise my three children.
—ANNE MARIE, 38

We were very active in our church, and after he died, all of the people we knew through church continued to be there for me. The church has many activities and those activities kept me going. There were so many people in the church who had positive attitudes; it helped me to realize that my life didn't end when my husband died.
—KATE, 79

The best advice I can give a widow is to go to a support group at a church. Learn about God. This helped me realize we all have one commonality: death. No matter who we are, we will all die. God has a plan, and it helped me to realize that.

—MARTA, 36

I had a spiritual foundation, and that helped me cope. I learned that people who struggle the longest after losing someone they love are those who doubt their faith. I believe in the soul. I believe that matter is neither created nor destroyed.

—JANIS, 57

Several months after Roy died, I was in New York City and walked into a beautiful old church that was situated amid a row of modern shops. Organ music was playing, and I made my way to the middle of the church and sat down on a wooden bench. I listened to the deep sounds of the organ, and soon tears began to flow. No one said a word to me. I actually felt closer to that which we might call "the holy" in that New York City church than I had at my husband's funeral. I can't explain it, but it brought me comfort and—dare I say—healing.

Being widowed inspires many women to seek out a spiritual home or reconnect with a religion they may not have been involved with for some time. What if you are not affiliated with a place of worship and would like to be? We posed this question to Rich Harter, Director of the Office of Evangelization at the John Paul II Center/Archdiocese of Milwaukee. The John Paul II Center runs the Nazareth Project, which sponsors a Bereavement Ministry providing programs and support groups for those who are grieving.

"Widows are always welcome in the church," Harter says. "The key is to respond quickly in helping a widow connect her spiritual longing to a local church. The first step is to get her connected to a local parish, and we would accompany her through this process until she becomes integrated into the parish community."

A religious or spiritual community may not be for you. That's okay. There are plenty of alternatives, which we've mentioned here.

EXERCISE!

Martin Luther King Jr. said, "If you can't fly, run. If you can't run, walk. If you can't walk, crawl. But by all means, keep moving." We think this is splendid advice for widows. I happen to be a runner. In fact, Jim and I are both runners. To me, distance running is an interesting metaphor for my grief. I ran before Roy died, but after he died, I felt funny about signing up for long races. I thought, "Roy won't be there at the finish line. I don't think I can do it."

But I did go back to my early morning runs. During those runs, I'd sort things out in my head, things related to work or to my grief, and then I'd focus on my actual running. I'd say to myself, "Each step forward, never going back." As the weather got nicer, I started setting small goals, like running farther each time. This helped me regain my confidence, not only as a runner but also in general. Running is the ultimate metaphor, because during a race, runners never look back. We keep going. Sometimes we stop at the water stations or walk up the hills, but we keep moving forward.

I tried to deal with my grief in the same way. I knew I had to literally put one foot in front of the other. There were hills, and sometimes I had to slow down, catch my breath, and even walk up those inclines. But there were other times when I would conquer the hills without slowing down, just charging up it. After reaching the top, I would realize it was my confidence and strength that had carried me.

Obviously, when I did run races, Roy wasn't at the finish line. But knowing that I could complete another race spoke to me about my grief. I started to put my running and my grief together in a different way: I started running races for charities. Each step mattered, and I was able to focus on the cause. In some races, I would run and then donate anonymously to a charity; for other races, I would formally collect donations. No matter why I was running, the daily training and long miles of a race were all part of my healing.

I was taking care of my body. I was learning to listen to what it needed. And I kept going. I didn't always know where the road would lead, but I knew I had to stay on it. Grief is like this. We don't know what is coming around the bend. It may be beautiful sunlight, or it could be an unavoidable hill. You just take a deep breath, continue to place one foot in front of the other, and forge on. Your clothes are soaked with sweat and your face is dripping. You try not to blink because it will sting. Just stay focused. And whatever you do, don't look back. If you look back, it should only be to see how far you've come.

Here's how Christina, 61, puts it: "I find that working out hard when I am heading to that darker place helps a great deal. I do CrossFit and the workouts are tough; however, the camaraderie with others lifts me. There is nothing like a good sweat and a bunch of endorphins."

KEEP A JOURNAL

Writing in your journal without editing your thoughts can be powerfully therapeutic. It allows you to be completely honest with yourself. There's no need to worry about why you are thinking something; you simply write whatever comes to mind. The process may seem goofy if you've never done it before, but it can be extremely healing—and surprising. It gives you an awareness of where you are at this moment in time. Keeping a journal can also be a valuable way to record your memories of your husband. As painful as this sounds, it can be helpful to record them now, so that you won't forget.

Here are some suggestions for getting started on your journal:

- There are no rules. That means free form, literally. You don't have to worry about spelling or grammar.
- Try not to edit. When we cross things out, we stop the creative flow. Go ahead and just write. It doesn't even have to make sense.

* If you don't know where to start, you can write a letter to your husband. Again, don't edit; just let your thoughts flow.
* If you are really stuck, try writing about something that is not related to your husband. Turn to the middle of a book or magazine and read a few paragraphs. Then write about what you just read. The goal is just to start writing.

If you are looking for a deep, therapeutic journaling exercise, you can try answering the following questions:

* What have I learned about myself this past month or since the funeral?
* What did I discover or notice about my relationship with (fill in the blank, just not your spouse)?
* What did I notice about my sleep?
* What did I observe about my eating habits?
* Was there anything I enjoyed doing last week?
* What do I want to do in the coming month?

CULTIVATE DIVERSIONS

Other kinds of emotional support may come from things like hobbies, clubs, or meditation. We recommend meditation because it can teach you to be calmer and more relaxed and keep you grounded in the present. You might also use quiet time for prayer or reflection. Just set aside time to be gentle with yourself without being self-critical. Of course, you may not quite feel up to returning to an old hobby, particularly if it's one you shared with your spouse. On the other hand, rekindling an old interest or starting a new hobby might be great for quiet fun and relaxation.

For Michelle, 58, it was gardening. "One very important thing to me was planting my garden. Just getting out in the sunshine, feeling the earth between my fingers, planting pretty things that would grow and give pleasure to me and others. I transplanted one little white petunia whose roots broke off during the planting process. It seemed the plant was unlikely to survive. I threw myself into nurturing it, hand watering it every day, keeping the weeds and the other plants off it. It struggled for a while, then produced one flower, then another flower. By the end of the summer, it had a mass of flowers. I felt so triumphant about it. I gave my husband all the care I could and he didn't survive. But that little petunia plant survived."

WHAT WIDOWS SAID

Another important thing I did was stay connected to people. It would have been so easy just not to have gotten out of bed. I tried to plan a social meet up with someone—a lunch, a walk—at least every other day. I also traveled a lot. People extended invitations: come to our beach house this summer, come visit me in New York and we'll see a play, etc. I said yes to all of them. I learned to be comfortable driving long distances, though my husband had previously done most of the driving when we'd traveled. I enjoyed being with people who cared about me, seeing interesting places. Eventually I decided it was time to come home and settle down and face my identity questions. But while not traveling as much, I am trying to stay open to experiences. When people invite me to do things that are new to me, I say yes to things I might have said no to in the past. I feel like everything I learn and everyone I meet can help steer me to whatever identity I may eventually find as a widow.

—SAMANTHA, 47

I knew for a long time he was going to die. He had multiple ailments. But I had an awful lot of emotional support from my family and friends. I never sat around feeling sorry for myself because I had no reason to. Life is good. And life goes on. I have wonderful children and five grandchildren with two more on the way. I have plenty of family activities to keep me going. There was never a reason for me to think that my life has ended just because my husband died. I have a positive attitude.

—DEIDRE, 82

YOUR SUPPORT TEAM

Taking care of yourself emotionally should be a top priority during the first months of your widowhood. You will probably need help as you move through the phases of your grief. You'll need to have your wits about you (or at least most of them) as you reengage with normal life. That may mean going to a job, doing all the chores you used to do, and taking on the household duties your partner used to handle. If you were caring for an ill spouse or running the household, this may not be a big adjustment—in fact, it might be slightly less work. But in most marriages, there is a division of labor, and the surviving partner is left with all the work and responsibilities.

To ease the burden, consider putting together a support team—an unofficial group of people you can call on for emotional support, financial or legal advice, practical assistance (for example, with yard work or babysitting), and just friendly chitchat. Your support team could include people to help you make decisions about work, confer about your children—their friends, schools, summer camps, or college applications—and plan your future. In fact, almost any aspect of your life might benefit from expert advice. Whatever challenges you face, ask for help, seek support, or schedule a consultation. Remember that when you are highly stressed, as you surely will be for at least six months after your spouse's death, you should not make important decisions on your own. In the chapters that follow, we'll look at the major life issues you will face, and we'll show you how to create a game plan for the coming year.

YEAR TWO AND BEYOND

You may rely on your family, friends, and an informal support team for the first couple of years or so. In fact, as time passes, you may find that you are not so reliant on others for the same intensity of support as you were at first. On the other hand, grief and recovery is so individualistic, you may not experience grief or the symptoms of post-traumatic stress disorder (such as sleeplessness, crying, reliving images, guilt, and bad dreams) for months or even years after your husband's death.

If this delayed reaction happens to you, don't panic or think that you are behaving abnormally. You are behaving the way you need to behave. But it may be two to five years out when you will need counseling, therapy, or a new social support network. As we have said before, we now reiterate: If you need help, don't deny it or bury your feelings. Ask for what you need.

=== CHAPTER TWO TAKEAWAYS ===

- *You will experience emotions you've never felt before.*
- *Some of the bereavement emotions you are likely to feel include fear, anxiety, shock and disorientation, loneliness, sadness and depression, anger, guilt, and loss of identity.*
- *You may find Byron Katie's four questions and turnarounds helpful in dealing with troubling thoughts and feelings.*
- *Options you have in dealing with stress and other emotions:*
  - *Join a support group*
  - *Go to some private therapy sessions*
  - *Talk to friends or relatives*
  - *Find a religious community*
  - *Exercise*
  - *Keep a journal*
  - *Cultivate diversions*
  - *You may also develop a support team to help you in various areas of your life during recovery.*

Remember to read Chapter Nine, "Your Game Plan." It includes a fill-in chart where you can list your support options, important numbers, and the names and contact information of your support team. Or you can customize the same chart online at KristinMeekhof.com, where you'll find all the Game Plan tools in this book.

chapter three

navigating the legal system

wills, estates, and the probate court

I knew my husband had a will, but I didn't know where it was. Someone told me I had to go to probate court because I couldn't find the will. I didn't know anything about the probate court, and I didn't know who to ask about it. But I began to be afraid that I would have to move out of the house because it might be taken from me if I didn't have the will.

—MARY JO, 38

THIS CHAPTER WILL WALK YOU THROUGH THE LEGAL ISSUES you are most likely to encounter as a result of losing your spouse. Most widows are faced with the issues discussed in this chapter relatively soon after the death—when you are in shock and may be too disoriented to clearly think through all the implications of these legal matters. Some widows will know exactly where the will or the trust is and what the spouse's assets are; others may have no clue where they are or whether there even is a will or a trust. Some widows have to deal with very complex estates; others may not even need to go through the probate court. Some may be able to handle all of the legal issues on their own; others may need an attorney.

You may already have an attorney to help you, although others may be vulnerable to unscrupulous lawyers, executors, or family members. Your best protection, however, is a basic understanding of the legal process and issues. So, in this chapter, we will explain what you need to know about handling the will and the estate, and what you need to know about probate court.

Before we get started, it's important to make it clear that this chapter is meant to be a brief, general overview of some of the legal issues widows may encounter after the death of a spouse. We are not lawyers, and none of the information, advice, or content in this chapter is intended to be—nor should it be taken, interpreted, or used as—professional legal advice or counsel. It is also not comprehensive; many widows could find themselves in different situations that may not conform to what is covered here, based on their individual circumstances. Each state has different laws regarding spousal deaths, probate, and so on, so we strongly recommend that any widow facing legal or estate issues or questions consult with an estate lawyer or law firm to get professional advice on how to handle her individual situation. However, we did consult with estate lawyers and professionals to bring you the best possible information in this chapter.

JOINTLY OWNED ASSETS VS. ASSETS IN YOUR SPOUSE'S NAME ONLY

In general, the following applies: joint ownership or beneficiary designation of any assets you and your husband have trumps a will. What this means is that no matter what your husband may have put in his will related to the distribution of assets, anything that you owned jointly—automobiles, land, houses, savings account, stocks, bonds, collectibles, etc.—automatically belongs to you after his death. For example, if a savings account is in both of your names, that account belongs to you after his death. The same is true with a house. If both of your names are on the deed, it is your property after his death. Similarly, if he left life insurance policies or an IRA account and you are designated as the beneficiary on both, they belong to you, no matter what the will says.

Local laws differ somewhat, and terms vary from one state to another. For example, having both your names on a house or piece of property might be referred to as "joint tenancy," "joint tenants with rights of survivorship," or "husband and wife." Consult your local laws or municipality to determine what laws and terms apply to your situation.

The major problems that arise in these matters have to do with the assets in your husband's name only. Suppose he owned an antique automobile, which he bought and restored, and he is listed as the sole owner on the title. Or the house, which he owned prior to your marriage to him, was a solely held asset in his name—your name was not added as a joint tenant. You may have to go through probate court to transfer the title or the asset's ownership to you. Any creditor's claims or debts also may have to be satisfied before the property or assets can be transferred into your name. Again, states vary in terms of the priorities of creditors, so it is important that you get accurate information about how this works in your area. We recommend consulting an estate lawyer who is very familiar with your state and local laws.

WHAT WIDOWS SAID

I feel really sorry that I expected him to be healthier and more energetic in those days before we knew he was seriously ill and dying. I expected too much of him.

—CLARISSA, 61

After his funeral, I had no more funds in the accounts and the money raised was barely enough to pay the mortgage. When I met with his employer's human resources department, I was told of the benefits I was entitled to. However, during that meeting, I found out he had not updated his benefits and life insurance to reflect our marriage. He still had his ex-wife and son as his beneficiaries. I had to go through probate to get the marital portion of his benefits, pension, and life insurance. Probate took about eight months, but the judge awarded the house and half of his life insurance and benefits to me just in time to pay overdue payments on the mortgage.

—CECILIA, 43

Since this whole business tends to be confusing, here's some quick advice about what to do first regarding assets, wills, and probate court. The first thing you should do is try to identify all of the assets that your husband had, including Social Security, pensions, bank accounts, property, and so on. Identify which assets you jointly owned and which assets are in your husband's name only. Locate the will and any trusts. Locating and identifying these items will help you as you go through the following sections in this chapter.

WHAT IS A WILL?

A will is simply a document that indicates how an individual wants his assets to be distributed after his death. Joint ownership of assets trumps any asset allocation in the will. A will only governs what goes through probate, assets in the deceased's name only (more on that below). For example, let's say he declared in his will that he would leave $25,000 to each of his three children, for a total of $75,000 to be distributed to them. However, all checking accounts, savings accounts, and investment accounts are in both your and your spouse's names, and other assets in his name only total $10,000. That would mean that despite his intention to distribute $75,000 among his children, he didn't actually have that money to give. Legally, only those assets in his name only could be assigned to his children without your consent. You are also not obligated to come up with the other $65,000. If you had sufficient money in savings and investments to provide them each $25,000 as he intended, you could allocate that money to them, but you are not legally obligated to do so.

You should also be aware that if a person disinherits his spouse in his will, in many states the spouse may still have certain rights that overcome this. Consult with an estate lawyer if you have questions about this.

WHAT IS A LIVING TRUST?

A trust is an arrangement under which one person, called a trustee, holds legal title to property for another person or persons, called a beneficiary (or beneficiaries). A living trust is simply a trust you create while you are alive, rather than one that is created at your death. A person can be the trustee of his or her own living trust, keeping full control over all property held in the trust. On the other hand, a testamentary trust is a type of trust that does not go into effect until the person who made the trust (say, for instance, your spouse) dies. Usually this type of trust is made within a will—often to create a trust for minors. When a trust is included in a will, the will goes into effect immediately, but the trust is not actually created until after the death of the will maker.

The big advantage if your spouse had a living trust is that property left through the trust usually does not have to go through probate court. The disposition of property held in a living trust is controlled by the terms of the trust instrument. That is, the terms of the trust determine whether the property is distributed immediately or if there are conditions that must be satisfied before disposition—such as a child reaching a certain age. But a trust is not controlled by your husband's will, nor is it controlled by the intestacy laws (laws that determine who is entitled to the property from the estate under the rules of inheritance) of your state, and it does not become a part of the probate estate (more on that later). If the trust is set up appropriately, you will become the trustee following your husband's death. This gives you the power to manage all of the assets and property in that trust. Generally speaking, assets that are not in the trust have to go through probate. Again, consult with an estate lawyer for any questions or advice about trusts.

WHAT IF YOU DON'T KNOW WHERE THE ASSETS ARE?

You may not know if your spouse had a will or trust or where they're located. You may also be unaware of the location of other assets your spouse owned. If your spouse registered the will in probate court, you should be able to find it there. That said, most probate courts will not give you or any other person information about the will unless you present a death certificate. Then you are entitled to review it.

But what about other assets? In the age of the Internet, many investment accounts and even savings and checking accounts are only accessible online. To gain access to such accounts, you need passwords. Ideally, you can locate or figure out your spouse's passwords. But how can you figure out what the assets are and where to look for them?

Here are some hints:

* Contact the professional who did your most recent income tax return. Usually, this person will know what assets there are and where they are located.

* Look at statements that have been mailed to your spouse, both at home and at his place of business. Some people have their account statements sent to their office. Monthly or quarterly accounts often will include account numbers.

* If you can access your spouse's email accounts, review recent and past emails. Account statements are usually emailed.

THE PROBATE COURT

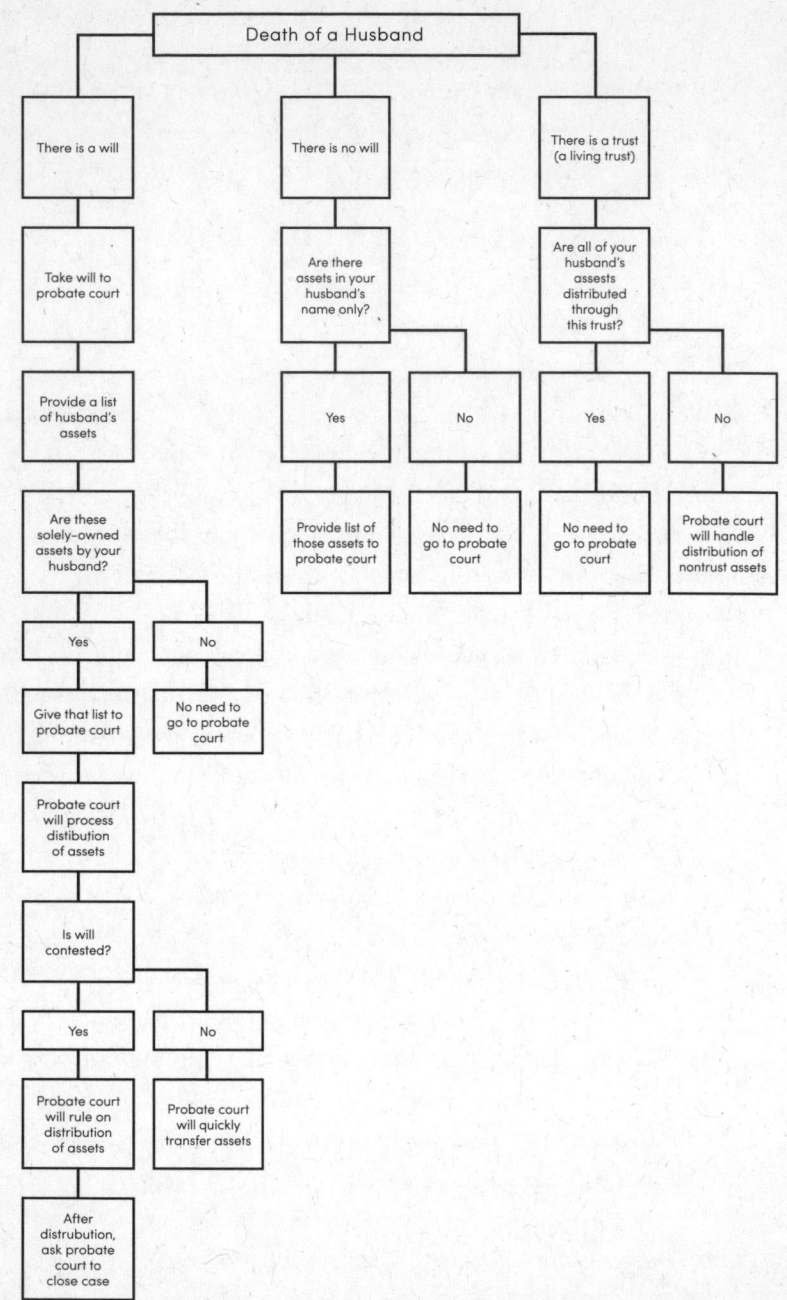

Death of a Husband

There is a will
- Take will to probate court
- Provide a list of husband's assets
- Are these solely-owned assets by your husband?
  - Yes
    - Give that list to probate court
    - Probate court will process distibution of assets
    - Is will contested?
      - Yes
        - Probate court will rule on distribution of assets
        - After distrubution, ask probate court to close case
      - No
        - Probate court will quickly transfer assets
  - No
    - No need to go to probate court

There is no will
- Are there assets in your husband's name only?
  - Yes
    - Provide list of those assets to probate court
  - No
    - No need to go to probate court

There is a trust (a living trust)
- Are all of your husband's assets distributed through this trust?
  - Yes
    - No need to go to probate court
  - No
    - Probate court will handle distribution of nontrust assets

THE PROBATE COURT

Many widows face one major obstacle related to legalities after the death of a spouse: probate court. Yet most widows—indeed, most people—don't understand what a probate court is and what it does or whether it applies to them. Furthermore, most widows do not know what has to go through a probate court. Here are some basic facts to get you started:

- A probate court is a county court that helps people handle such matters as wills, estates, conservatorships, guardianships, and the commitment of mentally ill persons to institutions designed to help them.

- The term "probate" refers to the method by which your spouse's estate is administered and processed through the legal system after he dies. The probate process helps you transfer his estate in an orderly and supervised manner. A state court called the probate court oversees the probate process.

- Probate is only required when the person (in this case, the spouse) dies owning assets that are in his name only. If this is the case and if there is a will, it is called a testate estate and the terms of the will govern what happens to his assets. If there is no will, it is an intestate estate and the laws in your county or state will determine who the heirs are and what their share of the estate will be.

- If there is a will, that will should be deposited with the probate court after your spouse's death, if it has not already been registered with the probate court.

- If there is a will and if there are assets solely owned by your spouse that are not in a trust, that will must be processed through the probate court. The probate court only deals with your spouse's solely—as opposed to jointly—owned property and assets, making sure they are distributed to the proper persons. When wills are contested, the probate court rules on the authenticity of the document and the mental stability of the person who signed it. The probate court also oversees the distribution of assets based on the instructions in the will, or if the individual died intestate, based on the law.

✳ Sometimes there is a trust, such as a living trust (because it was made when he was living) or a revocable trust (because it was possible for him to change it at any time circumstances or his wishes changed). Typically, any of your spouse's assets that have been entered in the name of the trust will avoid probate. However, you should discuss and review these with an estate lawyer to confirm that they do not need to go through probate.

WHAT WIDOWS SAID

For the most part, I didn't have any legal problems because all of our property was in both of our names. However, I was audited by the IRS after his death. That was because our house mortgage was in both our names. I didn't take his name off the mortgage and the interest was reported under his Social Security. I claimed to have paid it and the IRS audited me over it. I just learned the hard way that I should have taken his name off the mortgage immediately.

—LENA, 68

When Is Probate Court Required?

In general, probate court is not required unless your spouse had assets in his name only. If your spouse left a will, that will may or may not have been registered with the probate court prior to his death. If it was registered, the probate court may either have a copy of the will or know where it has been stored. If you find a will after your spouse's death, you must deposit it with the probate court in a timely manner or use it to probate his estate if he owned assets in his own name.

Once the will has been taken to the probate court and the

appropriate forms are filed to start an estate, you need to take a series of steps to probate that will.

How Does Probating an Estate Work?

Joyce Carol Oates's memoir features a chapter called "Probate," in which she writes: "Suddenly I'm worried—that the will isn't valid, or that my identity will be doubted. In my state of exhaustion I'm not able to think clearly, and could not defend myself or my interests."

You may feel the same way. If you do, we hope the explanations and the steps provided in this chapter encourage you to take the necessary action while helping you overcome your doubts and anxieties.

If there is property in your husband's name only, you must go through probate court. To do this, follow a series of relatively simple and straightforward steps:

1. File paperwork to handle your husband's estate in probate court. Go to the probate court in your area and ask for the appropriate paperwork to fill out, or access the forms on the court's website.

2. You may have to provide the probate court with a list of the assets your husband held in his name.

3. You may have to publish in a newspaper a notice to creditors to file any claims relating to debts your husband may have had and for which the probate estate (not you personally) may be responsible. If you were not a cosigner or the debt was not held jointly, they are your husband's debts. For instance, if he had a credit card that you didn't know about, and he owed $10,000 on that card, that is his debt—not yours.

4. Inform interested parties, including all heirs, as to what is going on. Relatives, such as children from a previous marriage or parents, may be considered interested parties under the law and need to be informed that your spouse's estate is going through probate, so they can provide any necessary information or take any necessary action.

5. Pay any valid debts and make required distributions to heirs and/or devisees.

6. Once all of the above is done, close the case. That is, once his debts have been paid from his estate and all interested parties have received their interest, you can ask the probate court to close the case. Once the case is closed, a very short window remains for anyone to make a claim against his estate. In some states the window of opportunity for an appeal may be as short as twenty-one days.

Having closed the probate court case on your spouse's estate does not mean that you will never have to think of or deal with it again. For instance, you will have to deal with income taxes before April 15 of the following year.

WHICH OF HIS DEBTS ARE YOU RESPONSIBLE FOR?

To help make this clearer, legally and technically, you are only responsible for debts you acquired together. For example, if you bought a house and both of your names are on the mortgage, you are still obligated to pay the monthly mortgage payments. If he spent time in the hospital prior to his death, and you both signed him into the hospital, as those bills come in—often months after he has died—you must pay those bills.

Most of us are good people and we try to be very honest and responsible in acknowledging bills and paying them. That could mean that you receive bills in his name after his death that you didn't know about. While technically you might be aware that you didn't run up a bill, you might still feel that you should pay it. It may be the right thing to do to pay his bills. It may be admirable to take on his debt. But you are not legally required to do this if those debts were not joint debts. We will address this issue further in Chapter Six.

WHAT WIDOWS SAID

My husband had recently leased a car before he died. I tried to return it, but I couldn't return it to the dealership; they said I had to call Honda. Then the company sent certified letters addressed to my husband saying they were going to repossess the car. It took me many phone calls to get this resolved so I could return the car.

—BETHANY, 55

WHAT IF HIS CHILDREN, HIS EX-WIFE, OR HIS SISTER FILE CLAIMS AGAINST HIS ESTATE?

This is where things can get complicated and heated disputes can occur. If you were a second wife and your spouse had children from a previous marriage, they may expect to inherit a portion of the estate. The will should designate his wishes in terms of inheritances. If it doesn't, and especially if you stand to inherit the lion's share of his assets, conflict may arise with other interested parties. Again, consult with an estate lawyer to determine what to do in a situation like this.

WHAT IF SOMEONE OTHER THAN YOU IS THE EXECUTOR OF HIS ESTATE?

In his will, your spouse may have named someone else to execute his estate. This person is usually referred to as a "personal representative." The personal representative will likely be paid a fee out of the proceeds of the estate. The personal representative may be a good thing—or not. It may be the spouse's intent that his personal representative will be fair and efficient in carrying out the provisions of the will. If the estate is large, having a personal representative may relieve the widow of the responsibilities of dealing with complicated financial and family issues. On the other hand, your spouse may have selected a personal representative because he did not trust your ability to handle the estate. If this is the case for you, you may find that your wishes differ from those of the personal representative. It may be a relief to know you can focus on the children and your grief rather than the administration of an estate.

INHERITANCES AND TAXES

The inheritances from your spouse (to you or other family or friends), which are sometimes referred to as "devises," will be designated in the will. An inheritance tax is a state tax that you pay (if you live in one of a handful of states that has such taxes) when you receive money or property from the estate of a deceased person. Unlike the federal estate tax, the beneficiary of the property is responsible for paying the tax, not the estate. However, as of this writing, only six states impose an inheritance tax. And even if you live in one of those states, many beneficiaries are exempt from paying it. Check with an estate lawyer to confirm whether you need to pay this tax or not.

Estate taxes are different from inheritance taxes. An estate tax is a type of death tax that is calculated based on *the net value of property owned by a deceased person on the date of death*, and the key difference between estate and inheritance taxes lies in who is responsible for paying it. An estate tax is levied on the total value of a deceased person's money and property and is paid out of your spouse's assets before any of the assets are distributed to the will's beneficiaries.

Before an estate tax is due, the value of the assets must exceed a certain threshold. These vary each year, but generally it's at least one million dollars. Because of this threshold, only about 2 percent of taxpayers will ever encounter this tax. An inheritance tax will only be collected if the estate passes to someone who is subject to the inheritance tax in the first place. Only six states currently collect an inheritance tax. But in all seven, as it turns out, a spouse is exempted from the tax when they inherit the property from another spouse. And children and other dependents often qualify for the same exemption, though in some cases, only a portion of the inherited property may qualify.

WHEN DO YOU NEED AN ATTORNEY?

Do you need an attorney? Some people will hire an attorney to represent their interests in probate court or help administer an estate. When we talked to Jill Koney Daly, an attorney and a probate register in a large Midwestern county, she said quite directly: "I definitely recommend you get an attorney if there is real estate."

Daly went on to explain the reasons behind her recommendation. "Most people aren't knowledgeable enough to prepare and file a deed and do all of the paperwork related to the transfer of land," she said. On the other hand, she pointed out, if property is in both of your names, you only need to go to the county's register of deeds to record the death certificate and to remove your spouse's name from that property. While this may not be important in the first few months, if you decide at some point in the future to sell the property, it will need to be in your name only.

Does your spouse's estate contain only common assets, like a house, checking and savings accounts or brokerage accounts, vehicles, and household goods? Things get much more complicated when an estate includes a business, commercial real estate, or any other asset that requires special ongoing handling. You will definitely want to consult an expert if you need to manage, appraise, or sell a business; you should not try to handle a job like this on your own.

WHAT KIND OF ATTORNEY SHOULD YOU GET?

If you require an attorney, you need one who is versed in probate and estate planning. But how do you find such an attorney?

A good place to start is to ask friends if they can recommend an estate planning lawyer they have used. Or you can go to the website of your state bar association, which may have a lawyer referral service that can assist you.

We strongly suggest that you do not find an attorney by responding to an offer of a free dinner at a restaurant in exchange for listening to an attorney's lecture on estate planning, wills, or the probate court. While lawyers who obtain clients through these strategies may be very skilled and competent, some are not. Some people have found that in such situations they have been pressured to sign on as a client or to sign an agreement of some sort. Also, don't randomly visit attorneys' websites. We've heard about lawyers who advertise on the Internet that they can help you "avoid probate" or that their specialties are bankruptcy and divorce. Those are not the lawyers you need.

We also caution you to be suspicious if your children or relatives want you to use their attorney. Even if you love and trust your family, you want an attorney that will unequivocally represent you and your interests.

Don't be afraid to interview potential attorneys and ask important questions, such as:

* What is your experience in the probate court?
* Have you done estate planning before? If so, how many cases have you handled?
* What is your fee?

You should be aware that rates for handling probate work vary considerably, often depending more on where you happen to be filing the probate case than on how complicated the legal work is. You can hire a lawyer to handle the whole probate case or just to help you do it. As executor of your spouse's will, you will not have to pay a lawyer's fee from your own pocket, although the inheritance is likely your money ultimately anyway. You can use estate assets to pay the bill before other inheritors get anything. Lawyers basically use three methods to charge for probate work: by the hour, a flat fee, or a percentage of the value of the estate assets. Many times the attorney will let you decide how you pay. For example, you may choose to pay the lawyer's fee of $250 per hour or agree to pay a $1,500 flat fee for handling your probate case.

WHAT SHOULD YOU EXPECT FROM AN ESTATE OR PROBATE ATTORNEY?

A competent attorney will ask lots of questions to understand your situation. In addition, you may be asked to sign an agreement to pay for legal services.

In general, however, the probate lawyer will ask for enough information to assist with the following:

* Locating and securing all of your spouse's assets
* Obtaining the values and appraisals of all of his property
* Preparing and filing all documents required by the probate court in a timely manner
* Collecting life insurance proceeds
* Rolling over and making appropriate elections with regard to retirement plans, including IRAs and 401(k)s
* Advising on the payment of your spouse's final bills and outstanding debts
* Keeping track of the estate checking account
* Determining whether any estate taxes or inheritance taxes will be due at the federal and state levels, and, if so, then determining where the cash will come from to pay the taxes
* Advising you on income tax issues
* Settling disputes among beneficiaries, heirs, devisees, and other interested parties

YEARS TWO TO FIVE AND BEYOND

The good news here is that legal issues—and this is the only place we can say this in this book—tend to be settled relatively soon after a person's death and thus will probably not catch you unawares in the future. That is, resolving estate matters and going through probate will likely be resolved in the first few months, certainly by the first year or so. No future legal complications will likely occur unless your spouse left you a business or property that you decide to sell later on. But you can make sure these do not catch you by surprise in the future by having an estate attorney check on the titles and partnership agreements related to real estate and your spouse's business before you are ready to sell those assets.

A FINAL WORD

Dealing with legal issues can be complicated and often takes more time than you would like. In general, just be aware that you usually cannot wrap up the legal process in a few days, and allot your time accordingly. It's crucial that you take the time to take care of these issues, regardless of how long it takes. We hope the steps in this chapter will help you do things in the right way, but again, always consult a lawyer if you have any questions or concerns about your individual circumstances.

One last piece of advice: Your spouse's will and how you will handle the will, probate, and your money involves confidential information. Be careful who you talk with about these matters and always safeguard that information as much as possible.

══ YOUR CHAPTER THREE TAKEAWAYS ══

- *A probate court is responsible for such matters as wills and estates.*
- *Probate court is not required in many situations after the death of a spouse; it is generally only required when the husband dies owning assets in his name only.*
- *If there is a will and it has not already been registered with the probate court, that will should be deposited with the probate court after your spouse's death.*
- *You are only responsible for debts that you acquired together.*
- *You will most likely need an attorney if your spouse owned real estate or a business.*
- *The kind of attorney you need is one versed in probate and estate planning.*

Remember to read Chapter Nine, "Your Game Plan," where you will find a checklist of the steps involved in settling the estate and a customizable contact list for legal advisors. You can also access these and the rest of the tools in Chapter Nine at KristinMeekhof.com.

chapter four

the widow's guide to solo parenting

As a mother of two young children, I worked hard at balancing the mommy role with that of being the primary caregiver. I was careful not to disrupt the routine my children had; I tried to make sure my family was there to take them to playdates, prepare dinner, and read bedtime stories when I had to work. At times, it was heartbreaking knowing my children were missing me and asking for me. I did my best to comfort my youngest son over the phone.

—CHELSEA, 38

I didn't try to hide my grief. I was there for them, and I wanted to let them know I was grieving. I didn't want my son, especially, to think he couldn't show his grief in front of me or others. I was aware he may feel pressure to be the man of the house.

—CHRISTIE, 52

KURTIS LAMKIN, POET AND MUSICIAN, SAID IT SO WELL: "Believing is all a child does for a living." Children live in their own world in many respects. Depending on the age of the child, make-believe and pretend are routine. That's why it is so heartbreaking to see a child lose a parent, regardless of the circumstances. With the loss of a parent comes a loss of innocence—and perhaps a premature entrance into adulthood.

While writing this book, we listened to many widows share their stories of how they broke the news to their children about the death. And then they told us how they integrated the loss into their family life. It was never easy, but we were amazed by their resilience. Many widows seemed to do this so well.

The ones who seemed to have a gift for this understood that while it's difficult enough for them to manage their sense of loss and their grief, their children will experience shock, sadness, and a range of other emotions about the death of their parent as well, and often in an entirely different way that requires special care. These widows recognized that their first obligation after their spouses passed away was to tell their children about the death of their parents (if their children didn't witness it). Perhaps nothing is so difficult for the mother of a young child as telling him or her that daddy has died. We assume that at this point you have probably passed this particular hurdle. However, if you should be reading this book soon after your spouse has died, this chapter will start off by telling you how you can best talk to your children about the death of their other parent and, from there, how you can navigate the new and complex world of single parenting.

HOW TO TELL CHILDREN ABOUT THE DEATH OF A PARENT

There is no easy or painless way to tell a child that his or her parent has died. The best way is to simply be direct, honest, and straightforward.

It's generally best to begin by talking about aspects of the situation the child has already experienced or noticed. For example, you could tell your child about the death in this way: "As you know, Daddy has been very ill lately and he's had to go to the hospital several times. Last night, he had to go back to the hospital." Next, give the facts of the death. "The doctor just told me that Daddy died today."

Having said this, you should be prepared for their emotional reactions and their questions. If there are questions, answer them honestly and with just enough information to help them to understand what happened. And, of course, you need to be sensitive to their feelings, but, as always, honesty is the best policy. For instance, there may be questions about how he died and if he is coming home later.

If your child asks, "What happened to Daddy? How did he die?" you can respond with what you know: "Daddy was driving home from the office when he was in an accident with another car and he died on the way to the hospital."

A younger child may ask, "Will Daddy be home before I go to bed tonight?" To this kind of question, straightforward honesty is the best policy, as painful as it may be. You can say something like, "No, honey, Daddy has died, and that means he won't be coming home anymore."

Often, beyond these direct and relatively simple questions will be more complicated questions. Children may pose the following kinds of questions:

⌘ Why did God let him die?

⌘ Are you going to die too?

⌘ Why do people have to die?

⌘ What are we going to do without Daddy?

There is no one way to answer these kinds of questions. But your response should be honest, sincere, and reassuring. If you are a religious or spiritual person, you might draw on your faith or beliefs in responding to some questions. However, in general, your goal should be to help your children feel safe, secure, and hopeful about the future.

CHILDREN NEED REASSURANCE AFTER LOSS

After the death of a parent, children will typically start to worry about your safety as their mother, so they will need extra reassurance from you. You can respond to any questions about the possibility of your death with an honest but reassuring answer: "Everybody will die someday. But most people live to be very old. And I think I will live to be very old too. You will probably grow up and have children of your own before I die."

If your spouse died in an accident, your children may be less easily reassured. They could say, "You could be in an accident too, and then you'd die."

An appropriate response to this is to say, "Yes, that could happen, but I try to drive very carefully and I always wear my seat belt. I know it is scary to think of me dying, but you [and your sister(s)/brother(s)] are very precious to me and I will make sure I take good care of myself, particularly when I'm driving so that I don't get into an accident. I'm sure I will be here to look after you for a very long time."

The bottom line is children need to know they will be safe and secure after the loss of one parent. When their world has been jolted, they need sensitive answers to what they are really asking to help them regain a sense of stability. When they ask questions regarding the death or their grief or loss, think about the emotional need underlying their question, and make sure you answer that need. By being sensitive to their emotional needs, as much as to the actual question they are asking, you let them know that you will make sure they are safe and that you will be there to take care of them. This approach will ensure that they feel secure and confident about their future safety.

In all conversations with children, it's best to remember what parenting expert Eda LeShan said: "A child can live through anything, so long as he or she is told the truth and is allowed to share with loved ones the natural feelings people have when they are suffering." Some parents, who seem to know this instinctively, start talking to their children about the death of their other parent at a very young age. Meredith, for instance, was only thirty-three when her husband died suddenly of an enlarged heart. And her son was just ten months old at the time. "I just explained it to him about his dad and kept doing it as he became older," Meredith said. "If I was crying, I would tell him I was sad because I missed Dad. He seemed to get it at a very young age, actually."

When telling your child about the death of their other parent, offer comfort through touching, stroking, and hugging as well. Despite the fact that you may be in terrible emotional pain yourself, your child needs love, affection, and comfort at this time. Children also need assurance that the world will be safe for them. They need to know that you are not going to let their world fall apart (any more than it already seems to have) and that you are strong and capable. So it's important to be soothing, calm, and comforting (even if you feel like that comfort is what you need yourself). You could say, for instance, "I'm very sad and upset about Daddy dying just like you are, but I am strong and I will be able to take care of you."

Rita, a widow living in East Lansing, Michigan, said that when her husband died from acute leukemia, she had to be strong for her five children. "I didn't always feel strong, but they needed me to be strong—and so I acted like I was. And the more I acted, the stronger I felt."

But Rita also passed on some important advice. "Never lean on your children. Never lean on anyone to the extent that they can't carry on with their own lives." This is sound advice. Children need to lean on their surviving parent; it's not their job to be comforter or therapist for a grieving mother.

> My son had to do a time line for school and put five significant life events on it and explain to the class. It broke my heart. He took a copy of the funeral program and taped it to his poster board and shared this with the class.
>
> —RACHEL, 40

CHILDREN GRIEVE DIFFERENTLY THAN ADULTS

It is hard for most young children to mourn—or to show mourning like an adult would. While children may not always seem like they are grieving, they are—at least at times. Children as young as three or four seem to mourn the loss of a loved one. In fact, their comments can reveal their real feelings about their loss. That's what Julie found out after she became a single mom to six-and-a-half-year-old Liza. Julia still had a regular dinnertime, but Liza was very much aware of her father's absence and wondered what the point was.

"We aren't really a family anymore," Liza declared during dinner a few weeks after her dad had died. Julie noticed that Liza was looking thoughtful as they both were eating yet another bowl of boxed macaroni and cheese.

"I murmured something about reinventing our family with just us two," Julie explained to us, "but it felt false. Dinnertime had been a time when we were together, the three of us, eating Henry's carefully prepared food. Food was family."

It's more difficult for very young children to tolerate intense sadness or anger. Many young children handle the death of a parent through denial or by avoiding experiencing the loss. In fact, young children may pretend nothing has happened. As an example of this, they may say such things as, "Daddy's coming home soon" or "I don't want to go to bed until my daddy gets home." It's important to listen and to understand how they view the world rather than get frustrated or annoyed with this behavior.

When their statements indicate denial or a sense that nothing is out of the ordinary, view this as an opportunity to help your child face up to reality. You can respond by acknowledging the denial and gently restating the truth: "Daddy won't be coming home to tuck you in like he used to because he is dead. I know it's hard to believe because he used to be here every night to say good night and read you a story. We loved having him here, didn't we?"

> My son came to me today and said, "Kids at school ask where my dad is and I tell them he's watching over me." It is really hard for both of us coping with his death.
>
> —SHANNON, 38

WHAT IS LOSING A PARENT LIKE FOR A CHILD?

Younger children tend to mourn and display their grief in small doses. It is frequently small things that stick in their minds for a long time. For instance, when I was two weeks shy of turning five, my father died after a long battle with cancer. I was his only child. I still recall vividly how I felt at the time.

You never forget the night your father dies. That was in 1979 but even now, more than thirty years later, it seems like yesterday, and at the same time, it feels like a lifetime ago. My parents took me to church and to Sunday school as a child. I learned about miracles. In other words, I believed with childlike innocence that people could be cured of anything. So the evening we got the telephone call that my father was very near death, I remember praying during the entire car ride for my father. I was with my paternal grandfather in the hospital waiting room when my grandmother told me that he had died. I'll never forget the looks on their faces. My hope for a miracle ended.

The morning of the funeral, my mom explained that my father was in Heaven, and very healthy, and so I imagined him running. I had never seen him walk because he was confined to a wheelchair due to complications from the cancer. But knowing my father was healthy was actually very comforting.

Later, when my paternal grandmother died, it broke my heart. We were very close for many reasons. Over the years, she became my main connection to my father. I felt like I was able to get to know him through her, so I was devastated by her death. Both my paternal grandparents had one of their own parents die when they were young, so for many years, they were the only people I knew who had had a parent die.

But what was hardest for me about losing my father was that, as a four-year-old, my childhood belief in the possibilities of miracles was shattered by the death of my father. Christie Coombs, in an interview we had with her, said something similar about what was taken from her children when her husband was killed on September 11, 2001.

Christie Coombs's husband, Jeffery Coombs, was on the American Airlines plane that crashed into the World Trade Center. He was forty-two and Christie and Jeffrey had known each other for twenty-three years. Their children were ages thirteen, eleven, and seven at the time. Later, Christie said, "September 11 took away my children's security; their ability to trust when we, as adults, tell them we're going to be there for them; their innocent outlook on life. It gave them one less person to express the pride in their accomplishments that only a parent can feel."

For children, losing a parent is like losing their innocence. But having a loving parent who is constantly reassuring and capable of helping them feel secure is the next best thing to having two parents available.

GUIDELINES FOR HELPING CHILDREN COPE

Here are some guidelines for helping children confront and accept the death of a parent:

⌘   Encourage them to cry if they want to.
⌘   Allow them to talk about their thoughts and feelings about their other parent and his death.

Charlene's daughter was almost five when her husband died. "Melissa lived through seeing her dad's condition worsen as he grew weaker from the hepatitis," Charlene explained to us. "He was home for more than two years in our home, most of which time he was in a wheelchair, before finally succumbing to hepatitis and spending his last few days in the hospital. Melissa was able to see her dad in the hospital a day before he died and then later view his body at the funeral home. She also attended the church service. By letting her experience all of this, we have always been able to talk about him. We frequently sit down and just talk about what kind of a person her father was."

- ✳ Express your own sadness openly. You might say, for instance, "I know you miss Daddy a lot. I miss him too."

- ✳ Acknowledge and accept their feelings. They will be more willing to talk openly if they are confident that whatever they feel will be acceptable to you. A child might blurt out an angry feeling, such as, "I hate Daddy for dying and not being here anymore." An appropriate response would be noncritical, such as "Many children your age and older feel that way when their daddy dies. I guess I feel that way sometimes too."

- ✳ Don't dismiss or ridicule any feelings your child expresses. You can mirror back their feelings ("I guess you are very angry sometimes about Daddy not being here"), which lets your child know you understand and that there's nothing wrong with their feelings.

- ✳ Think of grief as another form of language and know that some children express their grief best through play, art, or even music. Encouraging them to explore these areas can help your children cope with the loss of their parent.

- ✳ Physical aggression can be another form of expressing grief. Some children act out their grief through activity or aggression. If your child becomes more aggressive in the weeks and months following the death, respond to it like you would a more traditional expression of grief.

- ✳ Don't forget the pooch. Comfort dogs were used to reduce anxiety in children from Newtown, Connecticut, after the 2012 tragedy there. If you're open to getting a pet, dogs and other furry pets can establish connections with children in a way people cannot, and can help soothe a child's fears.

* Don't expect it will be easy. Talking to your child about the death of their other parent also means you are talking about the death of your spouse. However, talking about it—no matter how inexpert you are at this—is better than not saying anything at all. Since I (Kristin) was just a young child when my father died, I recall that my mother's emotional distance and refusal to talk about my father's death, or even about my father, did damage to me. It was disorienting. "Surely," I thought as an adolescent, "she can't be the only widow who coped by remaining stoic and silent." As a result, I promised myself then that I would write about it someday, not knowing that I would do so as a widow myself.

YOU MAY NOT ALWAYS SAY THE RIGHT THING

While talking about events and feelings is good, don't expect that you will always say the right thing at the right time. Chances are you won't. But if you keep the following general ideas in mind, there's a better chance you will say the right things at least some of the time.

* Provide age-appropriate explanations of death. Children age six and younger cannot understand the full meaning of death. For example, they don't understand that everyone dies, and they don't comprehend yet that dead people do not come back to life.

* Reminisce about the good times with their other parent. You can review family photos or videos, recall vacations, or talk about the fun you all shared at times.

* Openly express your love and support for your child. They need reassurance that they are loved. This helps to establish that there is still security and stability in their world.

* Don't hide your grief. You have to be strong, but you can let them know that you grieve at times too.

* Explain your philosophical or religious beliefs and outlook. If your family is religious, your beliefs can help your children

better cope with death. Your own philosophy, which may help you cope, will also be helpful to your child. If, for example, you have a belief in an afterlife, you may want to talk about this with your child. Rosemarie, who had two children under seven when her husband was killed in an automobile accident, told her children that someday they would all be able to see Daddy again in Heaven. And Charlene, who you met a few paragraphs ago, said that a Christian message was conveyed during the church service at her husband's funeral. "In talking with Melissa afterward," Charlene said, "I tried to convey to her that her dad was now in Heaven, and he was finally free of pain and suffering."

* Be honest with your child. You can let them know how you feel, but if they ask you a question and you don't know the answer, tell them you don't know.

* Kids needs normalcy and stability. Christie Coombs recognized this after Jeffrey was killed. "I knew my kids needed normalcy, and so the Saturday after he died, we went to the soccer field for their games." She said that her focus was on getting back to a normal and stable life. "And for me that meant letting my kids make some decisions about activities in their daily routine, like playing soccer when some people might have thought it was odd to be having fun," Christie said.

* Ask for feedback. If you are not sure if your youngster is grasping something you are telling her, ask her what she thinks or if she understands. If he/she says no, try rephrasing it or approaching it in a new way.

* Know when your child may need professional help. If your child is exhibiting new and serious symptoms, such as aggressiveness, a drop in school grades, or extreme withdrawal, and these symptoms go on for more than a few weeks, you should consider professional help with a child psychologist or a child therapist.

DEALING WITH YOUR OLDER CHILDREN

Media strategist and former CNN producer Susan Toffler's story of loss can be described as "epic" because it involves an enigma wrapped in mystery. Her husband, Thierry Imbot, was forty-two when he married Susan, then thirty-two. He had deep political connections with the French and Chinese governments and worked in France and Asia. When she was thirty-eight with a high-profile media career of her own and two sons, ages two and nearly five, Susan and Thierry sold their home in the United States and were headed to France to live as a family in Paris. Susan was hours away from boarding the plane to Paris with their two children when she received word that her husband had fallen from a balcony and died. It instantly made Paris headlines because people suspected one of two things: political murder or an unfortunate accident.

Grief stricken and shocked, Susan made the trip to Paris to bury her beloved husband. She says that her children have "no real memory of their father." However, she has made it her mission to keep their father's memory alive. "He's in our heart and on our shoulders," she remarked in an interview with us. In the years since her husband's death, she has chosen to raise her children solo and shied away from dating. "I raised my kids by myself," Susan said. "I didn't feel a need for a dad."

The boys were raised with an educational background similar to their father's. They are fluent in French and English, and have dual citizenship. When they were in elementary school, she says she "pushed for her kids to have male teachers" and kept in close contact with her in-laws.

The boys, like Susan, were never told the reason behind their father's fall. She said her son, since he is now in adolescence, googled his dad and had questions about the circumstances surrounding his death. She recalls him approaching her. "I said to him, 'I've been waiting for you to ask me this very question.'" She says she was very honest and explained that there is a 50 percent chance their father was killed for political reasons and a 50 percent chance he fell. However, suicide was not the cause of death.

Older children, like Susan's son, may continue as they age to process their father's death in different ways. As children mature, they may develop a different understanding—both intellectually and philosophically—of death. For example, a discussion in school may lead to questions that seem spontaneous and out of place at home. They may show sadness over longer periods of time, and in general find it much easier to experience their sorrow and grief. And it is usually easier to know what an older child is feeling and what is going on in his or her mind—not that you always want to know what's on the minds of your adult children.

Bea and her husband had three children who were all in their twenties when their father died. "My eldest daughter had the most difficult time since she and her dad were very close," Bea said. "My middle daughter had a set of twins that were four months old at the time he died. She also had a six-year-old son, so she had to think about her husband and children. My youngest was my son."

It was her daughters who had the most difficulty with their father's death. "My girls were very spoiled and could get anything they wanted from their dad," Bea said. "After he died, I could no longer afford elaborate or expensive gifts which my husband had been in the habit of giving them."

Another area of conflict occurred when Bea started dating again. "My girls thought they had the right to have some say," Bea said. "My oldest daughter felt a year after her father passed away was too soon for me to start dating."

As children age, they are likely to have more probing questions about their father or the marriage. They may also be more outspoken in offering their opinions about you and their father—particularly if their father had flaws of which the children have become more aware as they get older (such as alcohol abuse, drug addiction, domestic violence, or extramarital affairs).

HELP BOTH BOYS AND GIRLS HAVE AN ACCURATE PICTURE OF THEIR OTHER PARENT

When a mother is parenting alone, she often will make a serious effort to fill the roles of both parents to make up for the loss. But no matter how competent a mother is, she cannot really be a father or truly take the place of a father—especially for boys.

This is what Theresa discovered with her five-year-old son, Jonathan. His father, Theresa's husband, died when Jonathan was just one year old. In effect, he never really knew his father.

"Jonathan, for a couple of years, has been asking where his father is and why he doesn't live with us," she said. "I try to give him information that I think he can handle about his father being dead. But I have found that when he is talking with his friends or his cousins that he makes references to grandiose and untrue exploits of his father."

For instance, Theresa explained, he will say that his father lives in Mexico or that he is an airplane pilot or that his father taught him how to do a particular thing. "Sometimes I point out to him that he is pretending and that he should try not to make up fantastic stories about his father," Theresa said. "But this has been going on for several months and I wonder if it reflects a bigger problem and not just a phase he is going through."

Parents like Theresa certainly understand that children need a fairly well-defined sense of who they are and who their parents are to feel good about themselves. When one parent—the father in Jonathan's case—has died, the child may try to understand and cope with that loss. Eventually, how they cope will affect how they feel about themselves, their views of adults, and the patterns that get established later in life. How the mother handles this, then, is very important.

Raising a competent, emotionally healthy child in this circumstance means not only handling the absence of the deceased parent, but also being aware of the identification process and the need for a boy to model himself after his father.

A mother must realize that a young boy will want to be "like Daddy," and this will be reflected in his fantasizing and pretending about who his father is and the special qualities he possesses. When Daddy is not available or the child doesn't know enough about him, he must make up things about his father, such as his being strong or handsome or living in an exotic place, such as Mexico.

One way for a mother to help her son during the early stages of the identification and modeling phase of development is to give her son as much accurate information as possible about his father's positive qualities and traits.

Here are some suggestions for helping a son or daughter get to know their deceased parent:

- Give positive but realistic and objective information about their other parent when they request it.
- Do not discourage their fantasies or their efforts to compensate, unless you have something better to put in its place.
- Talk to both boys and girls frequently about their feelings about their other parent.
- Always be truthful and open about the facts and causes of the death. But remember that children younger than six or seven cannot really understand the full meaning of death, especially its finality.
- Remember to talk about your spouse in detail. Although this may be painful for you, it will likely help you and your children in the long run if you can give a more complete picture of who their other parent was.
- Share photos and videos (if you have them) of their other parent. Give them photos they can have in their room. If you can put together what might be called a memory book, this can be very informative to show your son or your daughter what kind of a person their other parent was. A memory book might include not only photos but other memorabilia that suggests details of his life. Such a scrapbook could also include things their other parent wrote or articles written

about him, cards he sent, business cards, album covers he liked, or tickets to events he enjoyed (such as sporting events or theater performances).

DISCIPLINE AND THE SOLO MOM

Being the only parent after the death of a spouse brings challenges, to be sure. One of those challenges is discipline.

Perhaps all parents would agree that coparenting is the ideal, because it's great when your coparent can step in and take over. At times, every parent may become overwhelmed trying to cope with an issue we're not handling very well. When these issues arise, it's wonderful to have a spouse or coparent step in and say, "I'll handle this."

But when you're a solo parent, you're on your own. That other parent isn't there to come in as the relief ace. You're going to have to deal with any problems all by yourself. While this is tough, it's certainly not impossible. Obviously, lots of mothers have done wonderful jobs parenting after the loss of a spouse. Here, though, are some useful tips for being the sole parent and disciplinarian:

1. Trust your instincts. If you have fairly good instincts as a parent, and especially if you were raised by competent parents, trust that your instincts as a parent are fairly sound.

2. Be consistent. It's a cliché, perhaps, to say that as a parent one of the best things you can do is be consistent. But it is a valuable tool in your parenting arsenal.

3. Set limits. One of the things you can't do as a single mom is try to make life easy because your child only has one parent. Your job isn't to make life easy for your child; it is to make sure your child grows up with the best skills to be a successful adult. One of those skills is self-control. To help your child develop self-control, you have to set limits and be firm and consistent with those limits.

4. Monitor your child closely. We have always loved the title of a parenting book written many years ago. The title was: *Hold*

Them Very Close, Then Let Them Go. That, to us, epitomizes the task of a parent. Supervise and monitor children very closely in the early years, but as they get older and show they are using good self-control and judgment, you can loosen the reins a bit.

5. Be authoritative. Things go wrong when parents are either too lax or too harsh. The better course is to be an authoritative parent. Be firm, be strong, but don't be harsh, rigid, or overly controlling. There's an art to being an authoritative parent, and it's important to strive for this.

6. Don't be afraid to make mistakes. Part of being authoritative is to make decisions and stand by them. But in doing so, you are going to make mistakes; all parents do. Admit your mistakes when they happen and move on.

7. Keep in mind that discipline is about a whole range of options, not just punishment. The best parents don't think first about how they can punish when a behavior problem occurs. Instead, they think about teaching and bringing about change. Typically, children don't learn best from punishment; they learn from being taught. If you can think of yourself as a teacher instead of a disciplinarian, you will be an excellent solo mom.

8. Finally, maintain a sense of humor. You can take the job of parenting seriously, but don't take yourself too seriously. Parenting can be fun, and it's fascinating to watch your child grow and develop into a wonderful personality. Children often have a terrific sense of humor. Nurture this sense of humor, and you can share lots of laughs while you're guiding them toward adulthood.

My son wants me to do the things my husband would do, and I try but I can't do everything. It is really hard to try to be both mother and father for a boy.

—JEANINE, 41

A FATHER-SON/DAUGHTER EVENT IS COMING UP. NOW WHAT DO YOU DO?

You may be doing very well as a solo mother. It's difficult, but you actually enjoy being the only parent at times. There haven't been that many rocky patches—until your son comes home from Scouts and announces, "There's a father-son camping trip coming up and I'd like to go." Or, "There's a model car competition for dads and sons. I want to do it." Or, you daughter comes home and informs you: "There's a father-daughter dance at school. Can I go?"

How are you going to handle these kinds of situations?

It may not be easy to pull off, but you have options. For instance, there may be a male relative—an uncle, grandfather, or older cousin—who could pinch hit for you. Or, if you know the parents of some of your son's or daughter's friends, there may be a dad who is willing to include your son or daughter as well as his own.

I (Jim) remember that when my children were in elementary and middle school, I was often that designated dad for other parents' kids—both boys and girls—when a father was needed for a father-daughter dance or as a guest speaker at school. My kids didn't mind, and the other children's mothers were always appreciative.

Besides locating a pinch hitter, you can take on the duty yourself, even though you are a mom. Some mothers don't mind being the only mother coaching a boys' soccer team or being involved in a model-car racing event.

Instead of fretting by yourself over what you're going to do, you can involve your child in the decision. Would he or she feel bad if you take on the dad role? Or does she or he know someone—a relative, friend, or neighbor—they'd like to invite to be the substitute father—at least for one event?

Always remember that you have options. And working out a solution with your child will help maintain the kind of mother-child communication you will need as they grow older.

SIX COMMUNICATION SKILLS SOLO MOMS SHOULD PRACTICE DAILY

Perhaps one positive thing that comes out of your experience of being an only parent is a recognition of the importance of communication. If you are going to parent by yourself, you know that maintaining positive communication with your children, especially when they are adolescents, is essential to a happy and healthy family.

Not only do you have to communicate about their other parent to help them deal with the loss, but you also need to make sure they are coping with life. And the only real way of knowing how well they are doing is by talking to them and listening when they talk to you.

If a teenager develops a problem, most likely his relationships will have communication deficits. While most teens want to keep some part of their lives private from their parents, to be an effective parent, you have to teach—and practice—communication skills regularly, starting when your child is young. That's the only way you can be fairly sure you won't be caught unaware of what your teenager is thinking or doing.

There are six important steps to healthy communication. Live these steps starting now, and you can reduce the risk of your child keeping serious problems or concerns from you.

1. *Have an open-door policy.* Lots of teenagers have said something like this to us: "But I couldn't talk to my mother about that." And we always ask why not. Their answers usually came down to this: their parent maintained a closed-door policy. There were issues and problems that couldn't be talked about. Instead, encourage your child to come to you to talk about anything and everything. No question or problem should be too silly, too embarrassing, or too unimportant. When your child comes to you to talk, always take it seriously.

2. *Teach communication skills.* You want your child to put feelings into words. Teach him or her how to do this. Encourage them when they are frustrated or mad to tell you how they're

feeling. When they do use words to describe their feelings, reinforce this with praise.

3. *Have patience and be a good listener.* Patience is an important part of communicating too. It takes a lot of patience to hear what children are saying and to show interest using eye contact and giving appropriate responses. No matter how busy you are, take the time to help your child tell you what they are thinking or what's bothering them. And while they're doing that, listen carefully.

4. *Be responsive.* You don't have to solve every issue or give wise advice every time. Often children aren't looking for advice anyway. They need a parent who will listen, show they are interested, and respond appropriately. An appropriate response might be asking clarifying questions, supporting their plans to deal with the problem, or simply nodding at the right times.

5. *Be a positive communicator.* How many communications take place between you and your child every day? Dozens? Maybe hundreds? If many or most of your communications are negative experiences for your child (because you fail to listen, reject their ideas or thoughts, or make them feel like their problems are trivial), it may teach your child that communication with you isn't worth it. Use positive communication instead. Let your kids know you appreciate them coming to you to talk, encourage their plans or ideas, and support their efforts to talk with you rather than keeping things to themselves.

6. *Be honest.* You need to be very honest with your children. For instance, don't lie about the kind of person their other parent was. When they find out the truth, they will be mistrustful of you. It doesn't mean you should be brutally honest or reveal things they are not asking about; however, when they do ask questions, be as honest as you can. Similarly, do not make promises that you do not intend to keep or can't keep. You

should not, for instance, promise in the early months after your spouse has died that you will never date or get remarried. While it may be the furthest thing from your mind in the first year or two, you may feel quite differently a few years later.

If you follow these steps to healthy communication, your children will appreciate your willingness to talk about anything and they will learn to be good communicators with other people in their lives.

YEARS TWO TO FIVE AND BEYOND

Children will not necessarily show their grief during the first few months and then get over their sorrow. And, of course, as we have said previously, the same is true for you. Feelings or behaviors in your children may emerge in the future, often when they are in a transitional stage.

For example, as your child goes from preadolescence to adolescence, you may encounter new and different attitudes and behaviors. Are these due to the normal progression from one stage of development to the next? Is your daughter's attitude snippy because she is an early teenager and trying to cope with the normal issues all young teens have to face? Or is it related to some previously buried emotions related to her other parent? The same questions may arise with a son's behavior in early adolescence. Is he stealing, lying, not turning in schoolwork, or taking up with some friends you don't like because he is working on becoming a more independent and self-sufficient teen? Or is it because he is thinking about and missing his father?

Since these questions are not easy to answer, it may be necessary to schedule an appointment with a therapist or child psychologist. An expert opinion may help determine if your child's attitudes, emotions, or behaviors are related to the loss of their parent or if it is just a phase they are going through. Learning which it is will put you in a much better position to handle it appropriately.

Of course, as we mentioned earlier in this chapter, as time goes on and you are making your recovery, you will likely consider dating or remarriage. This can be upsetting for children and, as it turns out, it is more likely to cause turmoil and disruption for an older child (an adolescent or adult child) than for a younger child. Teenagers and young adults will frequently mix up their own developmental issues related to sexuality and relationships with your efforts to have new intimate relationships with other adults. When this happens, as it almost inevitably will, particularly if you were widowed at a relatively young age, be prepared to deal with it with open communication and honesty. If openness and family communication doesn't lead to a comfortable understanding, it may be necessary to seek out a third party—like a therapist, counselor, or religious leader.

Another issue that may come up in future years is your child's last name. If you switch back to your maiden name, or if you remarry and take your new spouse's name, your child's last name will be different. This may be upsetting for some children and teens. They may be embarrassed by having a last name that's different from yours. Again, you should deal with this situation by being open, listening to your child's concerns, and having a family discussion. Allowing them to decide which last name they use is often the best resolution.

As always, by being a good communicator yourself and encouraging open communication within the family, you can set a great example for your children. The issues that do come up will be more successfully handled when you show that you are willing to listen and that you respect their feelings and concerns.

CHAPTER FOUR TAKEAWAYS

- *There is no easy or painless way to tell a child that their parent has died. It's best to be direct, honest, and straightforward.*
- *Children grieve differently than adults.*
- *Encourage them to cry if they want to.*
- *Allow them to talk about their thoughts and feelings about their deceased parent and his death.*
- *Provide age-appropriate explanations of death.*
- *Reminisce about the good times with their other parent.*
- *Give positive, positive but realistic and objective information about their other parent when they ask for it.*
- *Do not discourage their fantasies or their efforts to compensate— unless you have something better to put in its place.*
- *You can be a great mother parenting solo.*
- *It helps to be a good mother if you use appropriate discipline techniques and if you practice effective communication skills daily.*

Remember to read Chapter Nine, "Your Game Plan," for checklists and advice. You will need a game plan for raising your children as a solo parent.

chapter five
friends and family
the good, bad, and ugly

"What's friendship, when all's done, but the giving and taking of wounds?"
—FREDERICK BUECHNER

"True friends get their measure, over time, in their effect on you."
—PHILIP YANCEY

"Friendship improves happiness and abates misery, by doubling our joys and dividing our grief."
—MARCUS TULLIUS CICERO

SOCIAL SUPPORT IS A CRITICAL ELEMENT OF HEALING FOR widows, and having a strong network of friends brings about faster recovery. In conducting interviews for this book, we were pleasantly surprised to hear how many widows told us that they survived the death of their spouses because of the wonderful support they received from their families and friends.

For instance, Marilyn, who was in her seventies when her husband died, told us very simply: "I had an awful lot of emotional support from my family and friends." She also said that she and her husband had been very active in their church prior to his death. "I had so many friends," Marilyn said, "I never sat around feeling sorry for myself. I had no reason to. With my children, grandchildren, and friends, life is good."

Jane, in her late fifties when her husband died from a heart attack, credits her family for her recovery. "I was lonely," she says, "but maybe that never goes away. After all, you figure you are going to grow old together—you know, the companionship you'll both share forever. But all three of my children were still at home when he died, and that helped a lot."

Pamela, after a thirty-year marriage, said that her relationships with her husband's family really did not change after his death. "If anything," Pamela told us, "my relationship with my brother-in-law improved. He and his wife call me more often, and after three years, they have remained a very important part of my life."

Other widows also echo the strong support they received from family members and friends. Ann said that a good friend who is in the real estate business helped her to find a new home and made arrangements immediately after her husband's death to let her stay rent free in a home she owned.

However, some widows, while acknowledging the importance of supportive friends, found their families less helpful. Some even faced hostility, anger, rejection, and spitefulness on the part of in-laws and other relatives. This is most likely to happen when you were in a second or third marriage for either you or your spouse, and if one of you had children from an earlier marriage.

> I felt like they treated my husband's death like a divorce. Slowly, the invitations to family gatherings ended. At first I thought it was my imagination, and then I would see things on social media. They had parties and dinners

that I wasn't invited to. My heart would sink every time I realized I wasn't included. I wasn't prepared for this loss too.

—VIOLA, 40

Often conflicts with family can escalate over money. Tonya married Earl twenty years before he died, and she was well aware that it was his third marriage. Before he died, Earl promised Tonya that she would be financially well taken care of if and when something happened to him. What he didn't tell her, and perhaps didn't know, was that his children from his second marriage would try to get as much of their father's money as possible. They also thought they were entitled to the house he and Tonya had been living in when he died. They even attempted to evict her. At age seventy-three, Tonya didn't have the strength to withstand the hostility and legal wrangling. She finally asked her twenty-seven-year-old son to move in with her to help her with the expenses and to be supportive of her so she didn't feel like she was alone in her conflicts with Earl's children.

Danielle, at sixty-nine, had a different type of problem after her husband of almost forty years died. Her thirty-six-year-old son became very bossy and began making decisions for her. He forced her to move out of her home and into a senior apartment. "She was very unhappy in an apartment," Irene Swerdlow-Freed, PhD, her therapist, told us. "She felt lonely living in an apartment and she missed her neighbors."

During her career, prior to retirement, Danielle was in a management position with a large corporation and was comfortable directing other people. However, she was dealing with her grief and was vulnerable when her son stepped in to take over her life. "In therapy," Dr. Swerdlow-Freed said, "she was able to regain the strengths she displayed as a manager and began to reestablish herself as a more autonomous person." Danielle developed new friendships while renewing contacts with her former neighbors. She joined a senior center and spent time with supportive friends. She was able to take back her life from a son that she came to see as well-intentioned but misguided.

Relationships with in-laws can be tricky, and at times downright complex and stressful. This is just as true prior to the death of a spouse as it is afterward. How long you dated, the length of the engagement, and how soon you married after meeting can all play a part in determining what type of relationships you will have after the death of your spouse.

While you may believe everything was peaceful and tranquil between you and your spouse's family or relatives, the death of their family member can turn things upside down for all of you. One thing to keep in mind is that your spouse's parents, siblings, and children are also mourning a significant loss—just like you are. And out of this mourning, fears and anxieties may arise. And those fears and anxieties may be real or simply imagined.

YOUR SPOUSE'S DEATH CREATES MANY LOSSES

This chapter is perhaps the most difficult one for me (Kristin) to discuss. Within months of Roy's funeral, his older brother died. I flew to Florida to attend the funeral and get emotional support from his family. Unfortunately, from my perspective, much of this hoped-for support faded quickly after Roy's and his brother's deaths. Even more sadly, my husband had predicted that this might occur. Soon after we found out that his cancer was terminal, I remember crying and asking Roy if I would be alone. He looked at me with deep pain in his eyes, put his arm around me, and said, "I'm afraid you may not get what you want from my family." He then gave me the names of other loved ones he felt I could trust.

Now the loss of support from Roy's immediate family didn't mean I was sitting home alone during all the holidays, because I had my own family. But the diminishing contact with his family was a secondary and very painful loss. Before Roy died, there were some tensions with some of his relatives, but I still believed I would always be a part of his family. The disconnect with them wasn't immediate. It occurred gradually, which was even more painful. Could I have handled things differently? Absolutely. For instance, I could have been more open about feeling alone and overwhelmed. And because I was feeling lonely and isolated, I declined to attend some family events. I hated the painful reminders that Roy wasn't there to go with me.

If I could have worn a T-shirt with a big red heart on it that said "Forgive Me" to all of the family events, I would have done so. The first two years especially were filled with awkward and strange conversations. In the face of grief and everything else, I was a mess. I did the best I could to show up at family events, write thank-you notes (when I could remember), and reply to emails. Who knew I would struggle so many months after the funeral? Who knew I would be haunted by Roy's words so many years later?

Grief is not for the faint of heart. As you know, it is filled with disappointments, and that includes the loss of relationships. After the death, you do not know what kind of relationships will remain, especially your relationships with your spouse's family and friends. You may hope for certain things to occur and for people to reach out to you, but you don't know exactly what will transpire. This, however, is certain—you will be hurt all over again in some of these relationships. You will feel wounded and want to give up, but as soon as you realize this too is part of the grief cycle, you will be able to start healing. If I had accepted this earlier, I think it would have lessened my pain.

WHAT WIDOWS SAID

His family was supportive, but now I barely speak to them; we've just fallen out of touch. Sometimes I think they blame me for not keeping in touch. I miss their support but not their drama.

—SHERRY, 52

As mentioned, your spouse's death will result in many losses, and your relationship with your in-laws is often one of those losses. Some widows are lucky enough to enjoy close relationships with in-laws after their spouses die, but many, like Sherry, Viola, and me, do not. If you find this happening to you, try not to make it into a catastrophe. If you start envisioning yourself spending holidays alone for the rest of your life, you will only generate panic and create further anxiety. Remember, you have survived the loss of your spouse and you can make it through whatever happens today. The important thing is to focus on this day.

As we recommended in Chapter Two, you may need a support person to help you recover from this secondary loss. (Make sure it's not someone who is part of his family if that's where the friction started.) This should be not only someone you trust, but also someone who doesn't judge you. Call on a friend, a counselor, or a religious leader for advice on how to handle a deteriorating relationship after your husband's death. Often, other widows are willing to step into this role. If no one close to you quite fits the bill, don't be afraid to send out an email, even if you feel it is reaching a bit, asking someone you haven't been close to to meet for coffee to discuss this. Other people can't solve your family dilemmas, but they can often offer insight and humor, which can help you deal with them in a healthy way.

Writer Anne Lamott, whom Kristin went to see at a lecture and book signings, had the following to say about what she referred to as "domestic pain." We prefer to think that it very aptly applies to the kinds of secondary loss we're talking about here:

"Domestic pain can be searing, and it is usually what does us in. It's almost indigestible; death, divorce, old age, drugs; brain-damaged children, violence, senility, unfaithfulness. Good luck figuring it out. It unfolds, and you experience it, and it is so horrible and endless that you could almost give up a dozen times. But grace can be the experience of a second wind, when even though you know what you want is clarity and resolution, what you get is stamina and poignancy and the strength to hang on."

What these words mean to us is that while you may be looking for resolution of some of the family issues that come up after the loss of a spouse, you may discover that, whether or not you work out the problems, the main benefit is the insight that you have more strength and resilience than you ever imagined. And that's essential sometimes in dealing with domestic issues.

Dealing with family strife is difficult. To maintain your mental health and reduce further anxiety, appropriate coping mechanisms for awkward social situations after your loss are key. This means you need to be realistic and only go with what you know for certain. For example, don't assume you are not invited to an in-law's or your spouse's friend's event because you are no longer married. If you find out you weren't asked, let someone know you wish to be included in the future, but keep it brief and simple. During these difficult conversations, it's easy to get upset and unleash your worries or frustrations, which only escalates the situation. Try to stick with the facts, mainly asking about the event and whether you can go. If it is truly an oversight, you'll know right away. It may well be that his family or friends simply didn't realize how important maintaining a close connection is for you. If it's not an oversight, don't try to force your way through a closed door.

"YOU WANT THE FAMILY PHOTOS BACK?"— HANDLING YOUR IN-LAWS AFTER LOSS

Megan was widowed at age fifty-five after thirty-three years of marriage. "My brother and sister-in-law were initially very fearful that I would move on and they would no longer be a part of my life," Megan told us. "I had to assure them that they would always be a part of my family."

Not all widows are as fortunate as Megan, however. Some find they are no longer invited to family events. This emotional stress is intense, and you may be waiting for a happy ending. Although this may sound harsh (remember, we promised to be straightforward about the realities of being a widow!), some families treat the death of a family member the same as a divorce and may no longer desire to have a relationship with you. This can come about for several reasons. For example, they may feel that because you aren't a blood relative, you aren't technically part of their family now that your direct tie to them (your spouse) is gone. Or they may feel awkward about including you in their events or not sure how to relate to you now that part of your common ground is gone. And there's always the possibility that they may not have liked you when you got married, but they tolerated you because you married into the family. Try not to take this personally; after all, they might not have liked anyone your spouse could have married and this may or may not be your fault.

You may be surprised by the deterioration of some relationships that you thought were stable and would be enduring. In fact, relationships with your late spouse's family can become tense and strained in the immediate aftermath of his death. For, example, your in-laws may want items back that they consider to belong to "the family." A friendship with a sister-in-law that was such a source of comfort and enjoyment while your spouse was alive may sour. Such a breakdown of a once-comfortable relationship may be related to the role of children, how finances (such as an estate or an inheritance) are handled, or when you begin dating again. To you, the deterioration or loss of a relationship may seem unfair—it was not a divorce and you did nothing wrong. Unfortunately, this is how it can unfold sometimes, and the loss of relationships and friendships—within and outside of the family—will often intensify the loss of your spouse.

And then there are the money issues, which so many poor widows seem to face. McKenna, 48, told us about her ordeal:

"After Blake died, my stepdaughter wanted everything—even my house," McKenna said. "She fought me in court for three years, trying to get as much as she could. It cost me more than $50,000 in attorney fees, and his daughter spent at least as much trying to get everything."

McKenna said that her stepdaughter wanted the furniture, the two cars, and a cottage. "It was a terrible ordeal," McKenna said, "and I ended up settling just to get it over with. Emotionally and mentally, it was exhausting and I could not continue the battle at the same time I was trying to get over Blake's death."

As McKenna found out, children from a previous marriage may feel they are entitled to more than perhaps what was left to them in a will. When it comes to money and the emotions attached to money, stepchildren and others may be willing to battle you in court for several years to get what they think should be coming to them.

Lisa was just thirty-four when her husband died after only three years of marriage. What Lisa learned after his death was that he had been spending a significant amount of money each month to help support his mother and his adult brother and sister. They had gotten used to this support and expected Lisa to continue to provide them money each month. When she stopped paying, they tried to claim items of value that belonged to her husband and attempted to take some or all of his life insurance. These battles left Lisa emotionally drained and she decided to move to another city and cut off contact with her mother-in-law and her husband's brother and sister.

MANAGING AND COPING WITH DETERIORATING RELATIONSHIPS

If you find that some of your relationships become fractured after your loss, be aware that your actions can contribute to deepening these breaks. Be careful not to overreact to the signs of deterioration. Although it is not fair that your spouse died and others are seemingly punishing you for it, overreacting will generate an intense amount of stress and will only make matters worse.

Try to look at his family's or friends' excuses for what they are: just excuses. If you start reading more into them, you will develop anxiety. You may be extremely sensitive to the slights, the veiled hostilities, and outright cruel remarks that may come your way, and you may have every right to be sensitive and easily hurt, but managing your own stress is also a priority. If you want to salvage the relationship or heal yourself, it's crucial to look at the risks you take when confronting people about a deteriorating relationship. These include further alienating yourself from them, feeling a sense of panic or depression when they don't respond with open arms and finally melting down because you got your hopes up only to be let down. Instead, have options available. Turn to those friends who are still there for you. Spend time with people who enjoy your company. That's so much healthier than brooding about the hurts and slights you've received.

DISAPPOINTMENTS AND LETDOWNS FROM FRIENDS AND FAMILY

C. S. Lewis writes, "No one ever told me that grief felt so like fear. I am not afraid, but the sensation is like being afraid." Sometimes, our biggest enemy is our own mind, more specifically our own thoughts and fears. This is especially true for widows who are struggling to keep up old friendships or deteriorating relationships after their loss. Our thought processes can often set us up for failure before an actual conversation takes place. They can go something like this: "I know I shouldn't be disappointed if I don't get invited or mentioned, but I really want to go. Should I say something? No, I don't want to appear needy. Well, I am needy—my husband just died. Why can't anyone understand how lonely I am?"

These thought processes can quickly spiral out of control, causing you to react to things you fear, rather than what's really happening. Recall in Chapter Two that we wrote about Byron Katie's work and her four-step process for turnarounds, a way of examining stressful thinking and turning it around—changing your unproductive thoughts into productive perspectives that can help you work through your fear, worry, or grief.

Turnarounds, according to Katie, are opportunities to experience the opposite of what you originally believed. A statement can be turned around to the self, to the other, and to the opposite (and sometimes to "my thinking," when that feels appropriate). You should find at least three specific, genuine examples of how each turnaround is true in your life, and then allow yourself the time and presence to feel them deeply.

While we can't guarantee this will work for your family and relationship conflicts, Byron Katie's work provides a solid alternate perspective in managing your relationships.

MANAGING YOURSELF AROUND OTHERS

You read in Chapter Two about what Joan Didion wrote about her life changing after the death of her husband. Didion wrote in her memoir, *The Year of Magical Thinking*, that she discovered that grief changes everything. It changes how you view even the most mundane of life's daily events.

If someone asks you "How are you?" you may take this quite literally and start telling them about how you are really feeling, sharing your misery and loneliness. But, nobody really wants to hear how awful your life has been since your husband died. In fact, your friends and relatives may decide that you are too emotional and unstable to be around. As a result, they will avoid you, which is not what you want. No longer will you be invited to all the parties and get-togethers. We're not saying you shouldn't be honest about your feelings or what's happening with others, but be mindful of how you present yourself to people. While it may be difficult to keep your negative thoughts and feelings to yourself, it's important to ensure you're not inappropriately pushing your grief on everyone around you as well. Grief is personal, yes, and no one can understand what you are going through, yes. But that's not an excuse to unleash your anger and sadness over your loss anytime, anywhere, and on anyone. To preserve your mental health, reduce further anxiety, and maintain friendly relationships with others, you must (and can) learn to cope appropriately. This might mean saving your anger and grief for your closest friend—or seeing a counselor or therapist; venting to a rabbi, priest, or pastor; or even keeping a journal or writing about your deepest feelings in a blog that you may or may not share with the cyberworld. Be sure to read the last chapter of this book for more about learning to cope.

WHAT WIDOWS SAID

In our circle of friends, I was suddenly alone. I was the odd man out. There was always an empty chair, just as if they expected George to show up. When I go out with couples, it feels bad when they are talking about what they are doing or where they are going next. Nobody wants to say anything about him. They don't want to say his name. They don't want to make me feel bad. But it's worse when they don't talk about him. It's like he didn't exist.

—MARCIE, 64

PROCESSING HURTS FROM OTHERS

Depending on where you are in the stages of grief, you may be starting to process your prior conversations with others. That is, you may vividly recall hurtful statements that were said to you before or after your spouse died. For instance, Becky, 41, recalled a friend commenting that Becky and her husband didn't seem at all compatible. "I could laugh it off at the time," Becky commented. "But it wasn't so easy to laugh off after he died and I was trying to put our marriage in some kind of perspective. I began to think that maybe our marriage wasn't as great as I thought."

And Ramona, 57, was obsessed by her sister-in-law's comment at Ramona's husband's funeral. "Maybe this was God's way of punishing him for the affair you two had," her sister-in-law said. Ramona couldn't get that out of her mind.

So, like Ramona and Becky, you may be ruminating over

comments from other people that you found unsettling. You may be thinking, "Once time passes, his brother will apologize for that cold statement." Unfortunately, some people may never apologize to you. The absence of their apology may intensify the pain, but it's important to recognize and accept that it may never come. You will need to decide how to handle this.

The good news is you have options. Some enter therapy to talk and sort out this kind of hurt with a neutral third party. Or, for example, if an in-law or family member said something callous or hurtful to you, you can choose to talk with someone else in your family about what they said. But this approach has risks, since your words may get passed on to the person you are talking about, which could result in further alienation from family members. As a third alternative, you could choose to completely disengage from the troublesome person. If you do this in a peaceful manner, there will be no confrontation and you can both move forward with your lives. Eventually, you and others will view the tension as a byproduct of grief over the death of your spouse.

A final alternative is that you could confront the person with whom you have a conflict. You might directly ask for an apology or ask why you are not being included in get-togethers with friends or family events or why you're being avoided. Be aware this could cause you more pain. Emotions tied to your spouse are seldom easy to handle.

Healing can take time, especially since it is tied to such a significant death. Mark Nepo offers this viewpoint in *The Book of Awakening*: "One of the most difficult things about healing from being hurt by others is how to put wounds to rest when those who have hurt us will not give air to the wound, will not admit to their part in causing the pain."

Amends may never come, but forgiving those who hurt you creates healing. Sometimes it is necessary to forgive just so you can be at peace.

YEARS TWO TO FIVE AND BEYOND

Relationships with family and friends are likely to change after the death of your spouse. This is to be expected. Although family and friends can be the source of your greatest and most precious support, the relationships you previously enjoyed may change. Recognize that your family and friends are going through their own grief after the death of a loved one. Time is often needed to sort out the friendships and relationships that will endure and those that will not to survive the loss of your spouse.

While it would be comforting to think that you only have to deal with your grief over the loss of your spouse, and that you will have the loving support of family and friends, sometimes the emotions and even the avarice of others get in the way. As we found in McKenna's story earlier in this chapter, a fight with a family member who wants to get their hands on money or property they think belongs to them can go on for years, making matters even worse. This certainly complicates the grieving, adding additional stress when you really should be recovering from your sorrow.

The good news, though, is that many family members and friends will be there for you from the beginning and hang in there with you for many years into the future. Feel thankful and celebrate and build those relationships. You are lucky to have such a wonderful and supportive cadre of people in your life. And eventually, as you heal, you will meet more supportive and loving people.

YOUR CHAPTER FIVE TAKEAWAYS

- *Social support is a critical element of healing for widows.*
- *Having a strong network of friends will bring about a faster recovery.*
- *Keep in mind that your spouse's parents, siblings, and children are also mourning a significant loss—just like you are.*
- *After your spouse's death, you do not know what remains. You may hope for certain things to occur and for people to reach out to you, but you don't know exactly what will transpire.*
- *You are likely to be hurt all over again by your family and relatives. When you accept that this too is part of the grief cycle, you will be able to survive.*

Remember to read Chapter Nine, "Your Game Plan," where you will find a game plan that spells out exactly what you can do to cope with your life. You can access checklists and worksheets not only in Chapter Nine but also at KristinMeekhof.com.

chapter six

facing finances without fear

I quickly found out about things I never knew before. They can freeze your credit card; they can cancel your health insurance if it's in your husband's name. I had to reapply for accounts in my name. I would end up talking for hours on the phone with people, having to repeat the same story over and over, sending out multiple copies of the death certificate. I tried to do it all alone and it was overwhelming.

—KAY, 54

Our finances were a mess, but I didn't know this until after he died. I had believed my husband was taking care of our investments and resources. As it turned out, he wasn't; he was more interested in spiritual rather than financial things. I had to try to clear up the financial disaster.

—MARY LOU, 57

MANY WIDOWS ARE NOT AS INTIMATELY INVOLVED WITH THE household finances as their spouses were, and they discover hidden debts that surface after the funeral. Some have no knowledge about investments and financial planning and now must manage the family assets. Others have never worked outside the home and for the first time must earn a living. Some widows are embarrassed to admit that they have no idea how much is in their savings accounts or what their assets are.

If any of these examples describe your situation (or something similar to yours), don't worry; we're here to help. In this chapter, we will delve into the major financial issues widows face during the first and second year, and we will explain what you are likely to face after the second and third year. This section features insights from widows plus expert advice from financial pros and financial planners who specialize in working with widows and their finances. However, we offer this disclaimer: the information we provide in this chapter is just guidelines and, of course, each widow's situation is unique. You may need to consult with an attorney, an accountant, or a financial planner to get personalized advice.

SO, WHERE TO BEGIN?

When your spouse dies, you have many financial issues to deal with. But where do you start? We know from Chapter One that you are in emotional turmoil. And we said in Chapters One and Two that you shouldn't make any major decisions or changes the first year. But some things can't wait until you are psychologically ready to deal with them.

We like to divide situations into three categories: red light, yellow light, and green light. Red light decisions are major financial issues you need to stop and get input on before acting. For example, whether or not to sell your home is a red light decision. Yellow light decisions are things that may need a little input from others but will not dramatically alter your financial status. This could include changing your cable plan. You may ask your friends what plans they use and if they are satisfied with them. Changing plans may save you money, but it will not break your budget if you make the decision without additional information. Green light items are things that you are confident that you can end or change without any additional input. An example would be a gym membership your spouse had but you didn't. You know that this will save you money and needs to be canceled.

CREATING A DECISION-FREE ZONE

For some widows, merely looking at numbers on an invoice, policy, or financial report can cause a cold sweat. Personally, at times, I recall being so overwhelmed with statements that I would just look at the first page of each document and walk away.

Two financial experts, Dr. Kathleen Rehl and Bryan Wisda, have worked with widows for years. They both suggest that widows give themselves a "decision-free zone" (a helpful term coined by Susan Bradley of Sudden Money Institute) during the early grief phase following the death of their spouse. This is a time when a woman's cognitive capacity may be negatively affected by stress and the accompanying emotional roller coaster surrounding her spouse's passing. In their practices, Kathleen and Bryan have met many widows who made important financial decisions when there wasn't an immediate need to do so. Making ill-considered financial decisions can have long-term negative effects. For example, rushing to take your husband's name off a joint checking account could mean that any checks that subsequently arrive in his name cannot be cashed or deposited.

A decision-free zone is literally a time during which a widow makes no new major financial commitments—especially those that are irrevocable. It is all right for a widow and her family members to gather information and take care of routine financial matters that must be resolved soon, such as making sure the bills are paid and collecting life insurance benefits; however, it may not be a good idea to take big new financial actions, such as investing that life insurance check immediately, during this time.

Another experienced financial planner who has worked with

widows is Christine Isham, a certified financial planner and president of Northern Financial Advisors. She says the biggest challenge facing widows is that often their spouses had been taking care of the family's finances and they just don't trust themselves once they are widowed. "They are afraid and feel that without their husbands, they are lost financially," Isham told us in an interview. Therefore, she adds, they may want to turn their finances over to somebody else.

Dr. Rehl says she has personally witnessed a widow, under duress, who was persuaded to make a significant financial decision. That decision had dire consequences and couldn't be reversed. Once the widow was able to fully appreciate the impact of her action, she was devastated. Rehl was astonished at what she considered the unethical practice of the financial salesperson who made a profit off this widow's inappropriate decision.

LOCATING ASSETS AND DETERMINING WHERE THE MONEY IS

Not only do you need to know what the family assets are, but you also must determine where they are. Sometimes there are hidden assets, and untangling another person's finances may be very complicated. If your spouse used a financial advisor, and you know who this person is, it can help to meet with them.

If possible, obtain a copy of your previous tax return. Bank account numbers, other investments, home mortgage interest, job expenses, and certain miscellaneous deductions are often listed here. As tedious as this sounds, you will need to chart everything. We've provided a chart in Chapter Nine to help you in this area. Part of getting control of your finances involves organization. Listing all the assets and where they are located on the chart will help you organize part of your financial picture.

All the information you need may well be in your home, but you may not know where it is or exactly what you are looking for. Check file cabinets, desk drawers, and safes. If your husband primarily used online banking to pay utilities and you know his email password, you can request a new password. If you aren't computer savvy, you may want someone to help you with this. Simply go to the utility website and log in using his email address, and then enter his email and request a new password. Generally, that new password is sent to his email. Once you receive the new password, you can reset the email address as well.

If your spouse worked, you can ask his employer's benefits department what investment options he chose. Employers often make matching contributions, and they will at least have the name of the investment company he selected. If you have a safe deposit box and home safe, you will need to open them. Some of the important documents may be contained in either place.

If your spouse was working and has an office, ask for access to his desk or locker. Many people keep their personal financial documents at the office. It may seem odd, but some people get in the habit of paying bills at work. Take a good friend with you; this could get very emotional, but it is something you need to do. Also, check his car. Some people keep important items under the floor mats and in the glove box; sometimes that is where you will find the checkbook. Similarly, if your spouse had a locker at a gym or anywhere else, ask to have it opened. Especially if the death was sudden, there may be unopened mail—in his gym bag, for example. And finally, check his clothing pockets, especially coats. Some people keep checkbooks, bills, or receipts in their suit jacket pockets.

Christine Isham has frequently faced this situation with widows. "If they or their husband have not been working with me before his death," Isham says, "I ask her to gather all the paperwork she can find and bring it to me. If she can't locate any paperwork or documents, I ask her to just bring in a recent tax return. I can usually track down a lot of the assets from a tax return; and I also check with the employers, present and past, for possible retirement assets."

DETERMINING THE BILLS AND EXPENSES

If you have absolutely no idea of your household expenses, it will be useful to go to the bank or your bank's online banking site (you will need a user ID and a password), and ask for at least the last three months of checking and savings account statements. This will give you an idea of any automatic withdrawals (for instance, for utilities and other payments and fees) that may be set up. Do not feel pressure to move any money around, just obtain the statements. If you feel pressured by anyone at the bank, explain that you are seeking counsel before making any additional banking decisions.

You can also obtain information about credit card debts by getting a credit report from one of the three main reporting companies, Equifax, Experian, or TransUnion. Various websites, such as AnnualCreditReport.com, can assist with this.

For many reasons, a widow's expenses will be high the first year after the funeral. You will most likely receive invoices for funeral, burial, and medical costs—and these can keep coming in for months. Do not throw anything away. If you do not understand a statement or invoice, ask someone you trust for clarification. If you do not have a clear idea what you are spending, log your expenses (there is a form for this in Chapter Nine). If this is too much to keep track of at this time, simply save your receipts. This includes receipts for things like your coffee, dry cleaning, postage, groceries, and children's music lessons. This will begin to help you understand what you spend on a weekly basis. There's no need to judge it at this point. The idea is to create an awareness of your overall expenses.

Also in Chapter Nine is a form to help you to create a budget. Budgets are not set in stone. They can—and often need to—be adjusted from time to time. Expenses that can't be anticipated do occur. Believe it or not, one widow we spoke with had to pay a huge medical bill for her dog after it was hit by a car. She was living alone and her dog was her main companion. This was emotionally devastating and the vet's bills were enormous, but she couldn't think of living without her dog after already losing her husband.

You may start getting calls from collection agencies or debt collectors for bills you didn't even know existed. According to Sally Balch Hurme, who wrote *Checklist for Family Survivors: A Guide to Practical and Legal Matters When Someone You Love Dies* and works as a senior project manager with the AARP Health Law Education team, if you get calls from anyone saying that you or your spouse has a debt that needs to be paid, you should not give out any personal information, such as Social Security number, address, or bank account number. Furthermore, do not give out information about other family members or your spouse. "The only question the debt collector can legitimately ask," writes Hurme, an attorney, "is who has legal authority to pay the deceased person's bills. Do not answer any other questions, even if the caller sounds friendly or helpful. Do not agree to pay anything until you have checked with the executor or your lawyer."

If your spouse was ill for a long time, was taking costly medications, or had expensive medical procedures, the medical and hospital bills can seem like a financial tsunami—one that never ends. But be sure to pay yourself first. Make sure that you and your children have a place to live. The task of sorting through medical paperwork is too difficult if you are also worried about finding a new home. Next, you will need to save everything. You may see the same dates on different invoices and assume they are the same bill for the same service. This is not necessarily so. I know from my experience that I had to actually make piles on my dining room table because Roy received inpatient, outpatient, and hospice services. Sorting out different bills for different services or procedures was difficult.

Third, do not panic. Dealing with bills, especially medical and funeral bills, can be overwhelming, but this problem isn't going to simply go away. Just use the steps we provide for you and the forms in Chapter Nine. Fourth, get a notebook and take notes on every phone call you make or receive. You will start to make phones calls to ask if things are covered by insurance. It is impossible to remember everything. So get one notepad, start with the date, and literally log every contact. You may not get something resolved on the first phone call, but you will have a record. Finally, do not be afraid to ask for an appeal. I had several large medical invoices that weren't going to be covered. I made copies of them and asked the doctors for help. One doctor not only wrote a letter to support my appeal, he called the insurance company directly.

REMAIN OPTIMISTIC

You have good reason to be optimistic while engaged in the daunting task of dealing with medical and funeral bills. Maggie, a widow we got to know, called her husband's primary care doctor's office, and they didn't even realize that her husband had suddenly died. She explained that he fell ill, and she called an ambulance to transport him to the hospital. He died less than forty-eight hours after being admitted to the hospital. Maggie's husband had been seeing his primary care physician weekly for his diabetes, and this involved copays. Maggie asked if she could begin to make payments because she couldn't afford to immediately pay off the balance. To her surprise, the office took note of the previous payment record and wrote off the balance. "I couldn't believe it," Maggie told us. "I was stressed for days thinking about making the phone call and then they wrote it off. That was a godsend."

It is not uncommon to have no idea of the total amount owed to a hospital until several weeks or months after the funeral. Five months after Meredith's husband died, she found herself with over $75,000 in unpaid medical bills. "I had to swallow my pride and have a fund-raiser," Meredith said. The money raised, though, did make a significant dent in the expenses.

WRITE IT DOWN

Throughout this book, and especially in Chapter Nine, when we give you specific guidelines for your Game Plan we encourage you to write things down, keep lists, and make charts. The reasons for this are practical. You are going through an emotional crisis. You have many issues to deal with (financial matters are only one of these areas), and you cannot be expected to remember everything you may need to track. Earlier in this chapter, I told you about my red light, yellow light, and green light system. Let's return to that. Remember that red light decisions are those for which you should stop and get more input and advice before proceeding. Yellow light decisions are not so serious. You may consult with an expert if you choose, but making the decision on your own won't have devastating consequences. And green light decisions are those you can easily make entirely on your own. The following are seven areas to think about in deciding which items fall into red, yellow, or green categories related to your finances. Write down your answer to these questions:

1. Consider aspects of maintaining your home. Write down the monthly cost of your mortgage, utilities, condo association fees, garbage collection, cable, homeowner's insurance, and needed repairs or maintenance.

2. What are your other expenses? Write a list of your monthly and quarterly bills that will include auto insurance, cell phone fees, medical expenses, computer fees, car payments, and so on.

3. What real estate or property taxes are you responsible for? Make a list. If you don't know what your taxes are, you can find out by contacting your county assessor's office or recorder's office. You can usually get the information you need online. A good website to use is publicrecords.netronline .com. You will need the complete property address to obtain property data. Your taxes may be included in your mortgage payment, and you can determine this by reviewing mortgage statements for the past year.

4. Exactly how much income do you have coming in each month? Do you know what money will be coming in? Is it income you can count on? Make a list of all steady income and total this amount.

5. Do some calculations: Add your total income. Add your total expenses. With a calculator, subtract your monthly expenses from your actual monthly income. This will give you a true picture of your situation.

6. Is your home your biggest expense? Do you have enough money coming in to continue living there? Ask yourself why you want to stay in your home. Are you under pressure from family members to keep the house? Should you reduce costs by moving?

7. If you can afford to stay in your home for a period of time, put that decision on hold.

FINANCIAL STRUGGLES

It would be great if every widow were well-off or had significant assets she could use to handle medical and hospital bills, funeral arrangements, and the monthly household expenses. But the reality is that for most widows, this is just not so. While we talked to some widows who received large inheritances or significant insurance settlements and were left comfortably well-off, many others we talked to were struggling.

For instance, there is Ciara. When her husband died early in 2014, Ciara, at age forty-three, had not worked in several years. She and her husband had decided she should stay home to care for their children and for him during his long illness. "Although I believed his death was due to a service-connected disability, I could not get military benefits," Ciara told us. "Also, I have found it impossible to get another job so far. We are behind in our utilities and the power company is threatening to cut off our power. I just don't know what we are going to do."

And Cheryl, 29, related that financial problems started immediately after her husband's death from a massive heart attack. She quickly exhausted the funds in the bank accounts, but still had thousands of dollars in debt. "I was pleasantly surprised when his coworkers and friends pulled together and raised money to cover some of my bills. But after the funeral, I could not make the mortgage payment each month. For the first time in my life, I had to apply for state aid to help us survive."

What do cash-strapped widows do? How do they handle the inevitable financial problems and crises? Where do they turn for assistance? That's what this chapter is about. Using the realistic assessment of your assets and liabilities (which we hope you have done by following our suggestions above), you can begin to make some critical financial decisions. However, you may be entitled to benefits of which you are not aware. We will discuss how to find those benefits in this chapter. Any benefits you have coming to you may be crucial in helping you stay in your home or make rent or mortgage payments.

HOME SWEET HOME

Having a place to live is a top priority. But there is more to consider. The marital home is a significant and tender reminder of a shared place that holds memories. For many widows, it is a place where we feel we belong. For me, our home is where Roy received hospice care and died. He desperately wanted to be released from the hospital and "go home," and I felt the same way. Because of the memories our home held for me, I was very reluctant to leave. But I had to look at it from a practical standpoint. I was now alone, and there would be just one income. And I lived a half hour from my job. I had to think about what was best. Sure, my emotional connection to this home was important—but so was making ends meet and doing what was best for my psychological and financial well-being.

All widows need to consider three basic questions about the home:

1. Can you afford to stay there?
2. Is it in your psychological best interest to stay there?
3. Should you pay off the mortgage?

WHAT WIDOWS SAID

Now I live with my daughter in California. I had to leave my apartment, my cats, and my friends. I'm sleeping on her couch. I'm looking for work, but I don't have transportation so I need to find something close by, which limits me. The only jobs I can find are far away from where I live. I've been through a lot of hard times in my life but this has been the hardest.

—TISH, 44

CAN YOU AFFORD YOUR HOME?

If by doing the exercise we suggested above, you found that you can afford to stay in your home, then—as we wrote—you can put any further decisions about the home on hold. If you can't afford to stay in your home, continue reading this chapter for more advice about that looming decision.

The harsh reality is that for financial reasons, some widows will have to sell their homes. Moving to a smaller home is a painful, stressful transition and can cause additional worry. While grieving, it is an enormous task to even think about it.

Jamie, 63, who had been married thirty-five years when her husband died from cancer, was cash poor. "My husband wasn't able to work the last few years he was alive because of the cancer, and we had so many unpaid medical costs that we took out a second mortgage. When he died, I knew that I'd have to sell our home, but I didn't want to and I didn't want to ask my children for help. I couldn't sleep knowing I couldn't pay the bills. I had to take sleeping pills, and finally I had to move in with my son and his wife for a while."

Molly's husband tragically took his own life in their home. She didn't feel comfortable living there with the children. "I sought out mortgage brokers and experts. We couldn't see how I could maintain the house, so eventually I walked away. I felt bad, but even the experts told me with my circumstance, it was okay. There was no life insurance and I had to ask my friends to help me find a job."

But you may be like Sherita, who was forty-two when she was widowed. "At first, my financial situation actually improved," Sherita said to us. "I suddenly had a large infusion of cash thanks to gifts and the insurance money. I was able to use that to finish the remodeling on our home that my husband had begun before his death. It was a blessing to not have to worry about money for those first few months. Suddenly I had the ability to just go get whatever it was the kids and I needed. The grieving process would have been so much more difficult if we had had to add instant poverty to our situation."

There may be enough money from insurance or gifts (as was the case with Sherita) to make things comfortable for the first several months. However, the nagging question remains: What happens when the infusion of cash dries up? Will you be able to afford your home? If you can't determine that on your own by anticipating what income you will have, say, over the next five years, you may need the services of a financial planner. This will be discussed later in this chapter.

As we have written elsewhere in this book, you should not make any major decisions in the first year or so without expert advice. Here's what Candace, 55, said about that in regards to her home: "My brother made me promise I would stay in my house for a year and then decide after a year whether to move or not. I am glad I stayed in the house—as time went by, the house began to feel okay for one person. I had to refinance the house for a lower mortgage rate, but I am on a budget and that has worked out all right."

Christine Isham, in her role as a financial planner and investment specialist, has had to help widows face the question of whether or not to stay in their homes many times. "First of all," Isham says, "I ask them to put that decision off for a year or so. After a year or more, a widow will be in a much better position to make important financial decisions."

Isham says that, of course, if a widow has to move, then she has to move. But usually it is not a matter of money. "It's an emotional decision," Isham says. "After a year, they will know better how they feel and they can better face the question of what is best to do about the house."

In most instances, no decision has to be made immediately.

SHOULD YOU PAY OFF YOUR MORTGAGE?

If you have sufficient cash, you may consider paying off the mortgage. But should you do that?

Financial experts we consulted caution against it. Some suggest that widows consult a number of experts who can provide you with well-thought-out financial plans before paying off the mortgage.

One reason to give careful consideration to what you do about the mortgage, says Isham, is that by taking money from an account (say, an IRA or 401(k) left by your husband), you put yourself in a higher tax bracket, and you will end up paying more taxes. The idea behind an IRA or 401(k) is that that money is withdrawn after you are retired and when you are presumably earning less money; therefore, you pay less in taxes. "Pull out a large lump sum to pay off a substantial mortgage," Isham says, "and you pay taxes on that whole amount." Sometimes it is better to take out smaller amounts and make monthly payments on the mortgage because you pay less in taxes.

Some widows will need the tax break that paying a monthly mortgage provides. Others may need, in future years, the liquidity that cash and investment accounts may provide. A paid-in-full mortgage may be an asset, but it doesn't allow you to quickly convert that asset into useable cash.

Isham addresses one more aspect of this discussion that guides her as a financial planner working with widows. "I want to find out how much it stresses her to have a mortgage hanging over her head," she explains. "If it is keeping her awake at nights worrying about the mortgage, it might be less distressing to pay it off."

BENEFITS, INSURANCE, AND SOCIAL SECURITY

Certainly you will want to know if your spouse had a life insurance policy. You may be able to find this out from the HR department where your spouse worked, if the policy was an employment benefit. Otherwise, it will be a policy that your spouse took out and should be filed with other important papers and documents.

It may be more difficult to determine if other benefits are available. Some will be related to your husband's employment, but they could also be related to previous jobs or military experience.

Especially if you expect to rely on income from your husband's pension, Social Security, or veterans' benefits, you'll need to find out if you're eligible to collect these benefits now and how long they will continue in the future.

A one-time Social Security death benefit of $255 is payable to the surviving spouse if they had been receiving Social Security benefits or had been eligible to receive them. In most cases, you will not have to apply for this benefit; it will be sent within a few months.

If your spouse was receiving Social Security benefits, you should be aware that benefits for each month are paid at the beginning of the next month. You are not entitled to keep benefits paid for the month of his death. That is, your spouse must have lived through the entire month to be eligible for the benefit. So, for instance, if he died on July 15, the check that arrives in August must be repaid. If he died on July 31, you could keep the August benefit, but any others that arrive must be returned or repaid. If the benefit is direct deposited into a bank account, either the bank will freeze the amount of the benefit or the government will remove it from the account—possibly without notifying you. Be sure to take this into account when writing checks from your bank account.

Social Security must be notified about the death of your husband. You should call the Social Security Administration at 1-800-772-1213 to notify them. However, it is common for a hospital or nursing home to notify Social Security, so this may have already been done.

If you are eligible for Social Security benefits, or if you were already receiving benefits, contact Social Security to see if your monthly check will increase due to eligibility for a widow benefit. Your monthly benefit might change to a higher amount if your husband had the larger Social Security account. If his amount of Social Security was lower than yours, your benefit will likely stay the same. Social Security will only pay the highest benefit you are entitled to, and they will not pay the combined amount you received when your husband was alive.

FIND OUT WHAT BENEFITS YOUR SPOUSE RECEIVED OR WAS ENTITLED TO:

- To learn more about Social Security, go to the Social Security website (www.SSA.gov) or call 1-800-772-1213.
- Check to see if you are eligible for the Social Security Survivor Benefit and apply for the Social Security Widow Benefit.
- If you have children under the age of eighteen, you should apply for the Social Security Dependent Children Benefit.
- If you have previously worked and you are now disabled, you may be eligible for disability benefits.
- If your husband worked in the railroad industry at any time after January 1, 1937, railroad pension benefits may be available.

WHAT WIDOWS SAID

My husband was a professional musician for the previous ten years and unfortunately didn't pay enough into Social Security, so he didn't qualify for it. Because of this, he carried so much guilt the last three years of his life. He blamed himself for us losing everything and not providing for me. I told him I didn't care about the money. I would have sold my soul to keep him with me.

—LOIS, 38

MILITARY BENEFITS FOR WIDOWS OF VETERANS AND ACTIVE DUTY OFFICERS

As a veteran, your spouse—and you as a surviving widow—may be eligible for benefits from the U.S. government. Veterans' benefits are very similar to Social Security benefits. If your spouse was receiving veterans' benefits, you should contact the Veterans Benefits Administration and notify them of his death. You can call their toll-free number at 1-800-827-1000 or visit their website at www.va.gov.

They will help you determine whether or not any benefit payment must be returned.

MIGHT YOU BE ELIGIBLE FOR VETERANS' BENEFITS?

You may be eligible for Dependency and Indemnity Compensation or the Death Gratuity under certain circumstances. Both of these benefits are very likely available to you if your spouse died while on active duty.

Benefits may still be available to a surviving spouse and

children if your spouse was retired from the military.

To find out more about what you might be eligible for, go to www.military.com.

In some circumstances, you can ask for reimbursement of funeral or burial expenses, request a headstone, or have your spouse buried in a national cemetery or with military honors. In addition, educational benefits may be available for your children.

WHAT WIDOWS SAID

Financial issues started from the day he died, because he was the only one who worked outside of home. I had access to our bank accounts, but all accounts were in his name. Because he had been in the army for four years, the military covered most of the funeral expenses. But there were still many expenses the military and our limited funds didn't cover.

—CHERYL, 29

Although the benefits from the military, a company-owned pension, or Social Security may be a small amount, knowing that a certain amount of money will be coming to you every month can be comforting.

TRANSFERRING PROPERTY AND OTHER POSSESSIONS INTO YOUR NAME

You learned in Chapter Three that if you and your spouse jointly owned your house, bank accounts, and other properties, the transition will be relatively seamless. However, if the house, a business, or various assets were only in your spouse's name, you may have had to go through probate to have them put in your name. So should everything be changed over from his name to your name?

Dr. Kathleen M. Rehl, a widow and certified financial planner, writes in *Moving Forward on Your Own* that if a checking account is in both of your names, "Don't change your joint checking account name for a year or so because checks may still come payable to your spouse for some time. You'll be able to deposit these into your joint account."

Some things definitely need to be transferred from your spouse's name to your name. These include IRAs, 401(k)s, brokerage accounts, and bank accounts. Putting the house in your name is not necessarily an urgent matter, unless you plan to sell it and move. The same is true of an automobile. Your spouse's car should be transferred to your name, but this is only important when it comes to selling the car.

DEALING WITH YOUR SPOUSE'S BUSINESS

You may, as some widows do, find yourself faced with the daunting task of taking over your spouse's company. Should you sell it, run it, hire someone to run it, or simply close it? While we cannot tell you what to do, we can point out the options and offer guidance about where to turn to for more advice.

You should first go back to the red light, yellow light, and green light decision tree we discussed earlier in this chapter. Is deciding the future of your spouse's business a red light, yellow light, or green light decision? In other words, must you decide immediately what to do with it, or do you have some time to consider your options? If the business has a manager and can function for a time on its own, this issue might fall into the red light area. That is, hold off on making a decision now. In a year or so when you have had more time to deal with your emotions and seek professional advice, then you can make an informed decision.

If the business is a small business, solely dependent on your spouse (for instance, if he had a private practice as an attorney or psychologist), it might fall into the yellow or green light areas. It might not have any financial implications for you—it's simply a matter of closing the office (and, of course, notifying his clients), but it needs to be done in a timely manner so his clients and customers aren't wondering what happened when they get no response from him.

If it is a different type of business, and if you have the enthusiasm and time, it might be worth it to take the next year to explore taking over the business and then make a more informed decision at that stage. You will have some practical considerations, particularly if you have a career of your own and/or young children, regarding whether you can run a business, keep your job, and care adequately for them. Also, does the business have a strong staff and possibly a supervisor or manager who can run the business in case you can't be there all the time?

If you decide to take over the business for the next year and you weren't closely involved in it prior to your spouse's death, do you have enough time to learn about it? If there is no manager, do you need to fill that role yourself, or do you need to hire someone?

As with all major decisions in the year or so after your spouse's death, seek professional advice and guidance—and give yourself at least a year to make any important decisions regarding the business.

FINANCIAL PLANNING AND INVESTING FOR THE FUTURE

Widows need to learn about financial terms and where to go for guidance. If you are not experienced in making investments and handling the family finances, you need help. That generally means working with certified financial planners and investment strategists. The most important advice we can give you in this area is this: recognize when you are out of your depth and get the best professional assistance you can. It is not enough just to find a certified financial planner; you need one who is in tune with your situation and needs.

For instance, Bryan Wisda, a certified financial planner, who specializes in working with widows, says, "Most financial planners are ill-equipped to deal with a woman in massive grief. They're pushing her to make decisions. Widows need to seek out someone who has them in mind, not the bottom line. It's perfectly acceptable to ask the planner, 'How many widows have you worked with?'"

Wisda adds that it is appropriate and smart to ask financial planners how they make their money. If their earnings are based on a percentage of profit, you should be careful. It is often better to work with a professional who charges a straight fee—not one who makes a commission on what he sells you or gets you to purchase.

Family members who may seem strong and have definite opinions about what you should do with your money may not be good for you either. Wisda offers a cautionary tale about widows who bring their adult sons to the financial planning appointments. "The son is grieving his dad, but sons are action oriented. So they are ready to make decisions and changes. When they hear an expert telling them to do things, sons will often start acting on this, but almost nothing really needs to be done immediately."

Christine Isham gives similar advice. "Widows who are feeling overwhelmed or are paralyzed by the seeming complexity of the financial issues often are willing to let their family take over the finances. However, this gives the decision-making power to someone else to determine what is best for her. After she is feeling more confident and less overwhelmed, then she may find that others have made decisions that don't really reflect what she wanted done."

In seeking out financial advice, keep in mind that not every financial planner is a certified financial planner (CFP). Make sure you know what their certification is, how they have been trained, and whether they have worked with widows before. Bryan Wisda, for example, who operates Summit Wealth Management in Carefree, Arizona, is a CFP and NAPFA-registered financial advisor. The National Association of Personal Financial Advisors (NAPFA) is a national organization that provides support and education for personal financial advisors—all of whom charge a fee and do not take a commission for their services. That is, NAPFA members do not receive any compensation or other remuneration that is contingent on your purchase of any financial product.

WHAT WIDOWS SAID

We lived paycheck to paycheck prior to my husband's death, so we never had need of a financial planner. However, nine months after my husband died, I did finally visit with a financial planner.

—ERICA, 51

FINANCIAL PLANNERS AND FINANCIAL EXPERTS

Like Erica, many of the widows we talked to had never gone to a financial planner prior to the death of their spouses. Those who had were often wealthier or had a spouse who was in business or had explained or introduced them to financial planning.

It was common, we found, for women to go to the accountant who did their taxes and ask for help. Shirley, 55, did just that. "I had an appointment with our accountant just a month after my husband died. He helped me collect the various documents I needed."

So what can a financial planner do for you?

As Sarah, 48, explains, "I do not have a head for numbers and this financial planner was good at explaining things in a way I could understand. Ultimately, he helped me invest some of the insurance proceeds in sound stocks and bonds." That suggests two things an expert can help you with: (1) making sure you develop a better understanding of finances and investments, and (2) investing extra money wisely.

A financial expert can help you avoid various pitfalls. For example, Christine Isham suggests that an experienced and sensitive financial planner can make sure you don't rush any decisions. Furthermore, she points out, a financial planner can make sure you take care of those things that must be dealt with. "If a widow is paralyzed into inaction by fear," she says, "the financial planner can help you do what has to be done."

A good financial professional can help you establish your financial and investment goals and help you figure out your most comfortable investment strategies based on your personality and your financial needs for the rest of your life. Isham says that one of her major priorities in working with a widow is to help her become comfortable and confident in making financial decisions. She goes on to say that "I give them tasks that they can handle. I want them to make minor decisions at first, so that in a year or so they can make the major decisions."

WHAT WIDOWS SAID

Managing the finances was really difficult for me. I never liked handling the bills or our finances. But I found a financial advisor that I trust, and a friend who is good with numbers agreed to look at my accounts from time to time to make sure my advisor is on the right track. I also went to community college and took a course on finances, stocks, and investments. I never thought you could be friends with your banker, but I asked to meet the vice president of our bank. I told him my circumstances, and now I call him every time I have questions—it turns out that it really is all about relationships!

—CANDACE, 56

YEARS TWO TO FIVE AND BEYOND

You may do well financially during the first couple of years, especially if there was a life insurance settlement or you sold his business. It may be after the second or third year that the dust clears, so to speak, and you are feeling more settled and more confident. By that time, you should be in a better position to evaluate your finances and think more clearly about your own future. As we will discuss in Chapter Seven, you will have perhaps made some decisions about your employment or career options, and you will be able to think more lucidly about your own longevity and what needs to be done so that you have adequate money to live out the rest of your life without worrying about making ends meet financially.

At this point, you may need to come back to this chapter and read about financial planners and getting advice on investments so that you can be relatively sure you are handling your money in the best possible way.

But, after year two or three, another aspect of your life may dominate your thinking. That is, you may now be considering dating or remarriage. Although love and romance may be very important, key financial considerations must be taken into account when you have thoughts of moving in with a partner or remarrying. This may be when you really need to visit a financial planner to get professional advice. Read the next section to learn more about this.

GETTING REMARRIED OR FINDING A NEW DOMESTIC PARTNER

The U.S. Census Bureau reported that in 2011 the median age of widowhood was 59.4 for a first marriage and 60.3 for second marriages. It's a fact that women live longer than men. Indeed, half of women over age sixty-five will outlive their husbands by fifteen years. No matter how old you are when your spouse dies, you likely have many years of responsibility for household financial decisions ahead of you.

Financial issues come into play when you are thinking of getting remarried. Private pensions and Social Security can be affected if you remarry. Some traditional pensions will not continue to give survivor's benefits if you get married again. Accounts that are a hybrid between a traditional pension and a 401(k) may be more flexible.

In general, surviving spouses who remarry before age fifty-seven cannot collect veterans' survivor benefits, but those who remarry after age fifty-seven and were receiving monthly payments before remarriage may continue receiving those benefits.

For Social Security benefits, the law changed in 1979 and since then has allowed widows who remarry after age sixty to continue collecting benefits. Widows who remarry before age sixty forfeit their late spouse's Social Security benefits. But you and your new partner must also think about the risks of comingling money later in life, when long-term care costs and estate planning become important areas of concern.

You may prefer remarriage over simply living together for emotional or social reasons. However, if you live in a state that recognizes common law marriage, the state may still view you as married.

Here are several financial issues you should think about if you are considering remarriage:

* Your children from your previous marriage. If you have children who are attending college on financial aid, your new spouse's assets may be factored into the expected family contribution and change your child's financial aid eligibility.

* Your adult children. They may have concerns about how a remarriage will affect their inheritance or the family structure in general. You should discuss these issues openly with your children. Keep them informed, solicit their opinions, and help them accept what you intend to do.

* Survivor benefits. If you rely on income from your late husband's pension, Social Security, or veterans' benefits, find out whether you will be eligible to collect these benefits after a remarriage.

* Long-term care. Given the high cost of long-term care—a private room in a nursing home costs as much as $87,235 per year in 2011, according to a MetLife Survey—having a

partner who needs that level of care could strain both of your bank accounts. If you get remarried, you would need to spend down both spouses' assets before either of you would qualify for Medicaid (even if you have a prenuptial agreement stating that certain assets be kept separate).

Finally, as financial experts told us, when it comes to finances, widows have to take care of themselves. If you marry someone who has fewer assets than you, you may be jeopardizing your future security by combining your assets. "I want the widows I work with to have a plan in case something goes wrong in the relationship," Christine Isham says—and that means that her financial house is in order before committing to a new marriage.

RECOMMENDATIONS

When it comes to finances, what do widows recommend? We asked many of them what they would suggest to other widows. Here are some of the responses we got:

"Be aware of your financial situation before widowhood arrives," Sally Ann, 46, said. "I was widowed in my early forties and so obviously death can strike at any time. Husbands and wives need to have excellent communication about their financial affairs so that when death comes, the other is not left floundering."

Sally Ann went on to say, "New widows need to understand that they don't have to make investment decisions right away, no matter how pressured they may feel. It's enough to pay off debt, pay for the funeral, and provide for their immediate needs without deciding the future. I waited nine months before finding an advisor."

This is what another woman told us in a very direct manner: "Back off!" We were startled by this and asked her what she meant. "I'll never forget stopping at my insurance office to sign the life insurance paperwork," Rowena, 51, said. "The insurance agent asked me to visit with someone else in his office. I didn't know who he was at first, but it turned out he was a broker and I felt preyed on. He knew I had this large (to me, anyway) check and he was anxious to get his mitts on it!"

Rowena said she meekly said she wasn't ready to make any decisions. "But then he called me a week later. I didn't need or want this kind of pressure. Our lives as new widows are full of extreme stress and the last thing we want to worry about is what to do with our money right away."

Rowena ended up seeing a financial professional to get help investing her money. "He was hands-off and I appreciated that," Rowena said. "I didn't want a lot of phone calls. Just send me a quarterly report where I can look at the bottom line. If I call, then he should be available. When I finally got around to filing for my husband's pension a year after his death, I didn't understand the paperwork and this financial guy was more than willing to help me with it and advised me on how to take the payout. I was grateful for that."

We also asked for financial recommendations from experts. They suggested that before you write any checks, you consider that most women are emotionally connected to their money. "Widows may feel inclined to give money to their family," one expert said to us. "Remember that you can't solve grief with a check. You may be in a position to write out generous checks, but you may not yet know for sure how much money will be left over once all expenses are paid. Be careful not to commit to setting up a charity or a foundation in your late husband's name. It is usually best to wait a year before considering this because of the long-term consequences. If you feel compelled and are able to afford a monetary gift, you can always donate to an already established charity."

If you commit to a charity during the first year or so after your spouse dies and then realize it is not within your financial means to continue to give, you have the right to change your mind. If you feel uncomfortable making the telephone call, draft an email and have a friend read it over before sending it. Sometimes when you are dealing with money, it is easier to communicate by email. An email may feel less personal and give you time to consider what you want to say.

CHAPTER SIX TAKEAWAYS

- *Financial experts suggest that you give yourself a decision-free zone during the early grief phase following the death of your husband.*
- *Keep a log of your expenses and payments made during the first year.*
- *Create a budget.*
- *Use charts, lists, and logs to help you deal with the rather daunting task of taking over the family finances.*
- *Do not make any major financial decisions in the first year or so without expert advice.*
- *Contact the HR department at your spouse's employer to learn more about benefits to which you are entitled.*
- *You may need the expert advice of a certified financial planner to deal with your finances, your assets, and even your spouse's business.*
- *Research and consider the financial implications of getting remarried before making a decision with your next partner.*

Remember to read Chapter Nine, "Your Game Plan," where you will find checklists and charts to help you determine your income and your expenses, create a budget, and chart various financial records.

chapter seven

widow in the workplace

After my husband's suicide, I had to return to work full-time as a salesclerk. But over the next three years, I changed careers and become a yoga and meditation coach. It not only supported me, but it also saved me emotionally. Teaching classes helped me to be social and connect with other people. Now I wouldn't do anything else.

—HEIDI, 46

I didn't work much during our marriage because we chose for me to continue school and to be there for him, and it made it easier for his schedule. I am now learning to run all aspects of the house and make enough money to do so. I cannot bring myself to work more than part-time. I get overwhelmed and fear I will not be able to handle it.

—SOFIE, 28

AFTER DEALING WITH THE ISSUES IN CHAPTER SIX, YOU NOW better understand the scope of your financial responsibilities and needs.

You are ready to make realistic decisions about your working future. This chapter will address practical considerations related to your work and career planning. We'll offer advice from career guidance specialists and experts who help women make transitions.

In terms of work, widows fall into three basic groups: those who have never worked, those who worked at one time but have been out of the job market a long time (or are retired), and those who are currently employed. In this chapter, we will examine issues all of these groups face and help widows in each situation work through them.

TAKE STOCK OF YOUR EMOTIONS

It is difficult to make transitions in your life when you are overwhelmed by emotions. That's why we suggest throughout this book that you should avoid major decisions for at least the first year after the death of your spouse.

Vicki Lind, a career counselor in Portland, Oregon, said it this way: "I think that it is too hard to plan a career transition when one is still in the periods of shock, loss, and grief. Some women are not ready to work with me because they have not moved beyond their loss. Many widows have not gotten over thinking that they were going to be living happily with their husband on his retirement money."

Lind goes on to say that "some widows do not have the emotional resources to heal quickly. I think that these women need to be in crisis management mode and consider the option of seeing a community college counselor and choosing a training program. Or they can use their most marketable skills for the short term while they get emotionally and financially stable."

She points out that community colleges—as opposed to going to a career counselor or coach—are terrific for providing support for decision making through career-planning classes. "If a widow is too stressed by their new financial picture, it doesn't usually make sense to invest in a private career counselor," Lind says.

CONSIDER YOUR EMOTIONS REGARDING WORK

Once you have decided to go back to work or begun to work at a new job, you may feel overwhelmed and even angry. There is uncertainty in any work environment and dismissing your fears and anger could cause you further pain. What is often at the heart of your feelings is fear. You've lost a part of your life that can't be replaced and now you are feeling fragile. Taking these feelings to work or to the job search is normal.

Susanne Maurer, a Washington, DC-based licensed professional counselor and the founder and chief operations officer of Washington Career Services, has had many widows as clients. She points out that widows face the same challenges anyone returning to the workforce would encounter. "A widow, however, might need to find a job sooner rather than later since she is now the sole breadwinner," Maurer told us. "A sudden loss might also mean she isn't at all prepared for the job search or entering the job market as opposed to someone who has been planning to return to work. Just managing a job search after a devastating loss is a tremendous challenge."

For the widow, Maurer, who has worked as a career counselor for the George Washington University Career Center and has her MA in counseling psychology, explains she must try to focus on the search or in finding meaning in the job search. "In addition," she adds, "she has to manage her emotions during interviews and networking meetings."

THE DIFFERENCE BETWEEN CHANGE AND TRANSITION

William Bridges, author of several books on transitions including *Managing Transitions: Making the Most of Change* and *The Way of Transitions: Embracing Life's Most Difficult Moments*, points out that there is a difference between change and transition.

Change, Bridges explains, is a shift in the externals of any situation: a new boss, setting up a new program, a move to a new city, a promotion, or the death of a spouse. By contrast, transition is the mental and emotional transformation people must undergo to relinquish old arrangements and embrace new ones.

Transition, Bridges wrote, is "the process of letting go of the way things used to be and then taking hold of the way they subsequently become." In between the change and the transition—which culminates in a new beginning—is what he calls the "neutral zone." This is a period of chaos when all you know and can feel is that things aren't the way they used to be. When you get through this period, which for a widow would be the time during which you are grieving for your loss and still reeling from your world being turned upside down, you can begin to have a better sense of who you are now and what you want to do with your life. However, this period of chaos, the so-called neutral zone, may last for one or two years—maybe longer. It may be, as we found with some widows, that the neutral zone has continued for up to five or six years or more. It's then they are ready to move forward—to forge a new identity; to date or remarry; to get a new job. Or, in my case, to write this book.

A DELICATE BALANCE

Returning to work involves a delicate balance. On the one hand, you may wish your coworkers would completely understand how you feel and offer you support. On the other hand, you may hope they treat you in a normal way and just welcome you back. While you may want them to understand what you've been through and what you are going through, the truth, of course, is that most of them have never been widowed; only you went through this pain. This being said, you can expect that you very likely will not receive the type of support you are hoping for.

After about two weeks away from my job, I returned to work. I felt like a different version of myself. It didn't occur to me until I was walking into the building that this would be the first time I wouldn't be calling Roy during the day. My husband was my go-to person, and if I was in a sticky situation, he would always help me process it. He was always in my corner and this was a loss I didn't think about until I was back walking into my office. I also wasn't sure what my fellow office mates would say to me or how they would act toward me.

KEEP THINGS IN PERSPECTIVE

You've just experienced a horrendous loss and your world is broken, so this may not be the best time to seek out a completely new career. Many times, a new career involves learning a new skill set, developing new relationships, and ultimately putting your best foot forward. Even the most put-together employees have a period of acclimating to a new job position. You need to go easy on yourself as you make transitions in your life.

WHAT WIDOWS SAID

Unfortunately I had a struggle on two fronts: learning to live without my husband and getting work. In the three years since he died, I've had a whole series of work contract assignments. I even worked in the Middle East for a couple of months. That job ended abruptly, but that was good because I needed to go back to grieving.

—LUANNE, 53

WHAT IS YOUR WORK STATUS?

You may have decided after figuring out your financial picture (perhaps with the help we gave you in Chapter Six) that you need to go to work, or that you need to look for a new job, or that despite feeling like you need more time away from your job, you must return to work on a regular basis. It may be that you desperately need the income to pay the bills. On the other hand, you may have decided that you need to work to keep your mind occupied with thoughts not related to your loss. Or you may have reached a point where you've decided that you need a job (or to return to work) strictly for personal fulfillment.

Whatever the reason for your decision, you now have to seriously consider your options based on your skills, education, training, and abilities. Once you are clear as to why you are returning to work, seeking a new job, or looking to find a career for the first time, you should go about it in the most systematic and professional way as possible.

YOU ARE CURRENTLY EMPLOYED OR YOU'RE RETURNING TO WORK AFTER A RELATIVELY BRIEF TIME AWAY FROM A JOB

If you are currently employed or returning to work after a short period of time off, consider the following:

* How will you handle questions from coworkers about your situation?
* Will you be expected to immediately be at your peak performance level?
* What are your options if your current work is not likely to provide an adequate income?

WHAT WILL YOU SAY TO YOUR COWORKERS?

You are certain to get questions from your coworkers when you return to work after your spouse has died. As you return to work, you are battle scarred, but others won't be able to see the pain you are feeling as it's primarily emotional. Some people may be insensitive and ask awkward and inappropriate questions.

For example, some coworkers may stare at your ring finger, wondering why you are still wearing your wedding ring. Others may actually say such things as, "Well, you had a difficult marriage" in a strange attempt to comfort you. Still others may verge on complete inappropriateness and make such cringe-worthy comments as, "Don't worry, it won't be long until you are remarried." Some widows we talked to said a coworkers asked, "Didn't he leave you any life insurance?"

If you work in an office and have family photographs on display in your work area, be prepared for others to ask about your husband. It is better to return to work somewhat prepared for well-meaning and well-intentioned questions as well as those that are inappropriate or even bizarre. Anticipating what you may be asked, you should have a few crafted responses in your mind. Some handy ones would include:

❋ "Thanks for asking, but I'm doing just fine."
❋ "I appreciate everyone's kind sentiments and regards."
❋ "I needed to return to work to keep my mind off my sorrow."
❋ "You are so kind to ask about that, but I'm not ready to answer personal questions yet."

Of course, it is never easy to talk about your spouse's death, but the work environment can be tricky. Work parties and social gatherings are still considered work. You may feel more comfortable sharing something about your loss because you are at a restaurant or someone's home, but this is still the work environment. What is said Friday evening will still be remembered Monday morning. This means that being friendly with your coworkers is not the same as being their friend. If you share too many personal details, for example, about your spouse's death or your life with your spouse, don't be surprised if others know within twenty-four hours.

I have a rule of thumb you may want to adopt: If you don't mind what you share showing up on Facebook or Twitter, then go ahead and share. Otherwise, save it for your really close friends.

Social situations with coworkers can place you in a vulnerable position. I remember the first time I was at a holiday party with colleagues and someone I see every day said to me, "You must feel horrible. You have no one to share the holidays with." The comment was surprising and abrasive and absolutely unfounded. I spent the rest of the night avoiding the person and walking on eggshells, wondering if someone else would say something similar.

WHAT WIDOWS SAID

For me, going back to work was important. Knowing that I would just sit at home and wallow—or worse, drink myself into oblivion—I went back to work literally a week to the day after Jack died. People came by to give me hugs. On the anniversary of his death, I received a bag from an anonymous coworker with an electric candle and wax. Soon after that, a soda bottle with sunflowers showed up at my office (Jack loved to send me sunflowers). I honestly do not know how I would have survived without my coworkers. Now I actually hate weekends. I would rather be at work. There was a time when I believed that I was the one who had died and was in Hell...but my wonderful, fabulous coworkers...they showed me that there is still good in this world.

—JESSIE, 51

I returned to work after taking a week off. At work, I had three coworkers who had all lost their spouses within the past year, so we were supportive to each other—it was kind of a widows' club.

—CARLY, 56

WILL YOU BE EXPECTED TO IMMEDIATELY WORK AT YOUR PEAK PERFORMANCE LEVEL?

Work can be helpful because it gives you an opportunity to focus on something other than your loss. While nothing can fix your pain, your job can be a healthy distraction. Some widows who live alone find the social interaction with their coworkers beneficial, and the structure a work environment provides can be positive.

But there are a number of things to keep in mind as you return to work. The first is that you will very likely be emotionally and physically exhausted. You may be easily distracted, forgetful, disorganized, or scatterbrained as well—all common side effects of grief. At first, especially if you are a parent with young children, you will constantly be juggling your schedule to accommodate your work. If you have unresolved medical bills, you may have to make phone calls during your work time regarding these issues.

There's a strong likelihood that you aren't getting a good night's sleep, and this makes work a greater challenge. Some widows report having "widow's brain" which makes simple tasks difficult to complete. This can be frustrating, but keeping a sense of humor will make even work duties a bit easier. Practicing self-compassion is going to be important for you.

Sometimes I tell widows to try to look at their situation as if they are recovering from a very serious physical sports injury. You wouldn't expect an athlete to reenter the game performing at 100 percent. I think the same perspective can be given to work. For those widows who do go back to work, it is not unusual to feel that your coworkers or manager are closely watching you. Some colleagues are not certain how to treat you. They may or may not have attended the funeral or sent you a sympathy card. It is not your job to make others feel better, but others are curious how you will handle your grief.

If administrators or supervisors in your workplace are reasonable and sensitive, they will usually understand that you have suffered a significant loss and that it will be a while before you return to your optimal performance.

However, you need to be aware of the professional image that you are creating for yourself. While your employer can't discriminate against you because you are a widow, constantly talking about your loss at work could cause you to be perceived as overly emotional. This doesn't mean that you are about to be fired, but you could get passed up for certain projects or promotions. Managers want a stable and dependable workforce.

WHAT WIDOWS SAID

My company gave me lots of leeway following my husband's death. I was a manager and they really needed me and it felt better to be busy. But in retrospect I probably should have taken more time off.

—EMILY, 47

WHAT ARE YOUR OPTIONS IF YOUR CURRENT JOB IS NOT LIKELY TO PROVIDE AN ADEQUATE INCOME?

If your current work is not likely to provide an adequate income after your partner's death, you do have some options. For instance, you might consider some of the following to help your financial situation:

- You could sell your house in order to reduce your expenses. Or you could move to a less expensive apartment or condo.
- You could get a roommate to help with expenses.
- You could move to a cheaper city.
- You could plan to change jobs or change careers.
- You could consider going back to school for more education or training.

If you choose to try to change jobs or careers, read on in the next section. If you are satisfied with your present job, you may still discover some valuable ideas later on in this chapter related to setting goals and what Kristin discovered about herself from thinking about a second career.

WHAT WIDOWS SAID

I was working when my husband died. We got health insurance through his company, but that will end in a few months. Since I have two teenagers, benefits, especially health insurance, are a big deal. I could go full-time in my present job, but it would mean more time away from my girls.

—CAROL LEE, 39

KNOW WHY YOU ARE SEEKING WORK

If the best option for you is to seek a job or look for a new position, you should be clear in your own mind why you are choosing this option. You may not share all your personal feelings of loss during a future interview, but it is important to understand, for yourself and in case you are asked, why you are seeking a job.

Colleen Phillips, a business coach who works with women around the world, told us that if it has been a long time since you worked outside of the home, there are several things to look at. "First, you might consider identifying what you might like to do," Colleen, who was widowed at age forty, says. "What is an ideal career or job? What would the environment look like? What are your passions? What are you most interested in doing? What are the hours and commitment you want or are willing to put in? What are your strengths and development opportunities? How much financially do you want or need?"

She suggests you then write a résumé to begin your job or career search.

In constructing a résumé, keep in mind these essential questions:

What is my dream job? What can I reasonably handle? What types of work am I good at? What type of work environment is healthy for me? What type of supervision do I need? Is there any room for advancement at this company? Am I seeking this job so that I can gain experience and plan to move to another company?

Phillips adds that it would be wise to translate personal life experiences into transferable skills. "While not working, what were you doing? Were you a leader in a parent organization, charity, or church? Where do your life experiences indicate strengths in leadership, communication, teamwork, project management skills, and organization? You should leverage all of this on your résumé."

WHAT ARE REALISTIC GOALS TO SET FOR YOURSELF?

No matter your employment status or the reasons for your career decisions, you must make sure your goals for yourself are realistic and attainable.

Consider how long you want to remain in your current position before seeking new employment. You should have some idea how long it takes to apply for jobs and actually get hired. And you should be realistic about the qualifications and skills employers are looking for in the field you have chosen. In the following sections, we will help you do some reality checks when it comes to work.

CHANGING JOBS OR STARTING FRESH: HOW DO YOU GET STARTED?

Perhaps you have to earn money to support yourself, or maybe you need to get out and do something productive for your emotional health. The fact is that you need to go to work or get a new job. If you haven't worked before or in a long time, where do you start?

Susanne Maurer told us she thinks widows should start off with some self-assessment and awareness exercises. "Understanding yourself is the first stage in career development," Maurer said. "Ask yourself: Who am I? What do I like to do? Where might I like to do it? What are my top passions, my interests? What do I value? What have I been doing over the past several years that I can transfer to a job (and résumé)?"

Based on the advice we gleaned from Maurer and other career counselors, here are some basic ideas about how and where to begin looking for a job:

* Look at job hunting as your temporary part-time—or full-time—job.
* Don't set your sights too high. It might be necessary to accept a lower-paying job (even a minimum-wage job) to get yourself into the workforce or to get a foot in the door at a particular company.
* If you are a graduate of a college or a technical school, go back to that institution (even if it's been several years) and ask the alumni office or the college career center for help. Or ask about job fairs (which many college departments hold annually for undergraduates) so you can plan to attend.
* Consider applying for an internship.
* Network. Ask everyone if they know of any company that is hiring or anticipating a vacancy.
* Go to conferences, job fairs, workshops, and any other event where you can pick up a few tips and meet more people.
* Consider looking at nonprofit agencies. They may be seeking someone with your skills.
* Volunteer at a business or agency where you would like to work. You won't make any money to begin with, but you may be able to show them they really need you and should hire you.
* Sign up at a job placement firm or a temporary placement agency. You may only get short-term jobs, but you may also find a company and a job you really enjoy. And a company may find you and offer you a full-time position.

✳ Use social media to your advantage. You may have been skeptical of the practicality of the social media; however, some sites can be very valuable when you are job hunting. LinkedIn, for instance, can extend your visibility around the country and with people and businesses you would never be able to contact otherwise.

Perhaps the most important idea in the above list is that you need to reach out to people and network. More than a cliché, networking is a valuable tool. By talking to people, meeting and asking people for advice, and using social media to let others know you are looking for a job or a career, you will be maximizing your opportunities to find the job or career you want. "The widow needs to utilize her network—social groups, alumni network, anything that can help her both learn more about what she might want to do as well as put the word out that she is in the market," concludes Maurer.

You may end up taking a job you feel is beneath you. However, even though your ego may take a hit if you accept a menial job, remind yourself (perhaps frequently) that you have taken a job for which you are overqualified to get a start, build your résumé, or make financial ends meet. You can always keep looking for another job.

QUESTIONS TO ASK YOURSELF ABOUT WORK

- What type of work do I realistically think I can handle?
- Does my current skill set match the required job duties of this position?
- Besides a paycheck, what can I gain from working at this new job?

> ## WHAT WIDOWS SAID
>
> Going back to a workplace where I have seven years of employment and coworker friendships has felt more odd and difficult. They were supportive too, but I definitely feel like I don't fit in anymore. There are new faces there, so that may also contribute to the unsettled feeling I sometimes get. Going back is also another chance to sort things out in my head and heart. I've been seriously thinking of making another employment change. I feel somewhat bored in this old position. Somewhere to start fresh. A big factor in holding me back in doing so is not having my best friend (my husband) to talk it out with.
>
> —CINDY, 43

PROFESSIONAL CAREER COUNSELING

According to Susanne Maurer, a career counselor can support the widow at any point during the process of seeking a job or changing her career. "A career counselor," Maurer says, "is very helpful if she needs some extra support or someone objective to review her résumé or discuss job search strategies or options."

Furthermore, a career counselor or coach can offer career assessments—formal as well as informal—to start the process. "Career counselors also," Maurer points out, "usually have suggestions on how to network and create a job search strategy, as well as offer résumé and cover letter reviews and interview preparation."

Colleen Phillips indicates that a career counselor can help widows in gaining clarity, focus, and a plan. "Not only do career counselors help with résumé writing, interviewing, and negotiating a total compensation package," Phillips says, "but they can champion and challenge you to achieve what is most important to you now."

How should you go about finding a career counselor?

A good first step would be to do a Google search for career counselors in your area. But you can also go to the National Career Development Association at www.ncda.org or go to www.coach federation.org to find a qualified coach or a career counselor.

Maurer adds, "Just like with a clinical counselor, it's important for the widow to find someone she truly connects with."

GUIDELINES FOR YOUR JOB SEARCH

You've just experienced a horrendous loss and you may feel like you are experiencing an emotional free fall, so this may not be the best time to seek out a completely new career. Many times a new career involves learning a new skill set, developing new relationships, and ultimately putting your best foot forward.

A little over two years ago, I decided to pursue a freelance writing career. I started to write this book, and I wanted to expand my reach by writing more pieces. I continued to maintain my full-time job as a clinical social worker, and wrote during my evenings and weekends. That has been nice in the sense that I don't feel pressure to write all the time. However, there are moments when I feel pressure to leave my social work job and give everything I have to my writing career. Then, logic weighs in to remind me that I need a steady paycheck and health insurance.

During the past year, there have been times when I felt like I was in an ultramarathon with no clear finish line. I stop here and there to take breaks, refuel, and share my joys and woes, but I continue. It is surprising to learn who continues to cheer me on along the way and who, to my disappointment, departed from my cheering section. Some of the departures were unexpected. They came after I refused to compromise my integrity and do professional favors. For me, pursing a second career seems like that: an ultramarathon.

But why did I pursue a second career? Because I thought I was mentally tough enough to do so. After all, I had survived the unexpected death of my husband in 2007 and felt sharing my story could help others. Since starting this second career, I've learned many lessons by trial and error. Here are nine of them that I would like to share:

1. **Growth makes you vulnerable.** This sounds obvious, but I was surprised that the growing pains I've experienced often came as a result of being raw and open. In many ways, widows develop an acute sensitivity to loss. With this being said, rejection—either through an interview or something that happens at work—can be especially tough. All kinds of change seem to represent another kind of loss. We went through an earthquake that measured 9.0 on our emotional Richter scale. But we are still here. Adjusting to work—whether a return to a previous job or a search for a new one—is another significant change, and it is normal to feel vulnerable.

2. **Follow your gut.** I had a series of conversations with another very successful businessman. I met this individual through a writing assignment I did free of charge. Others criticized me for working for free, for cheapening "my craft," and their comments gave me pause. Yet something deep inside me told me it was the right thing to do. I was curious about the subject matter and pursued it. One result was that I was introduced to this wildly successful and gentle soul. His guidance and friendship is priceless.

3. **Check in with yourself.** After my conversation with this gentleman, I knew that I needed to reassess my approach to pursuing my second career. This wasn't anyone else's writing career but mine. In many ways, we all have our own job stress. We each have a goal line that we strive to cross. Learn to adjust as needed and pursue only one important goal at a time. In a real sense, you really do take it one day at a time.

4. **Reexamine your game plan.** You may feel that your plan is solid and able to withstand the test of time, but as new challenges arise, you may need to readjust it. I've learned to

have plan B formulated as I pursue plan A. This helps because it doesn't leave me feeling disorganized when things seem to fall apart. Most likely you never thought you would find yourself in this work situation. The one constant in life is change. You will need to adjust your own game plan numerous times. This is to be expected.

5. **Be careful who you listen to** (especially if they can benefit from you in any financial aspect). We all have blind spots, and when money is involved, we may be careless about who is giving us genuine advice. However, nuggets of wisdom can be tainted with dollar signs. Widows often say they feel like they are wearing a large sign on their back that reads FRAGILE. Some people will take advantage of this and have their own best interest at heart—not yours.

6. **Listen to your body.** Athletes often are told, "Listen to your body." A new career can physically and emotionally deplete you, and you will not be able to do your best work. Be sure to rest. Rest prevents injury. Being widowed is very hard on your body. You will notice physical symptoms that may need to be addressed. A study recently published in the journal *Immunity & Ageing* found that among the elderly, in particular, the recent loss of a loved one may leave a person more vulnerable to infectious diseases.

7. **Rejection happens.** Rejection is especially painful after your spouse has died because it is another type of loss. Understanding that sometimes we associate the loss of our spouse with other types of rejection can help us understand ourselves better and see why we might take rejection to heart. I remember I felt that at one point I was in the flow of many good things. I had been published numerous times and I assumed that I would be able to obtain a literary agent. I got rejected by the first agency I contacted. I was devastated. The same week, a piece I wrote was also rejected. I talked to my trusted friend, and he offered this piece of wisdom, "Kristin,

this is not how you are going to make your mark. It is just part of it."

8. **Practice gratitude.** I believe that gratitude is the answer to nearly every question. There has yet to be a situation that I've encountered in which I couldn't apply gratitude. It reminds us of what truly matters.

9. **Dance.** Remember to celebrate each goal or finish line you cross. There are several along the way. When you are able to do what you love most and experience joy, remember to dance!

═ YOUR CHAPTER SEVEN TAKEAWAYS ═

- *It is difficult—sometimes impossible—to plan a job or career change when you are not emotionally ready for a transition.*
- *If you are returning to your job after a brief respite, expect personal, inappropriate, and sometimes bizarre questions and comments.*
- *Don't expect that you will be able to return to work and work at your highest level of performance right away.*
- *If you decide to go to work for the first time or the first time in a long time, or if you decide to change jobs or careers, personal assessment can help you better understand your motivations.*
- *You may need professional career counseling to discover your skills or for support in achieving your career goals.*

Remember to read Chapter Nine, "Your Game Plan." It is where you will find exercises, charts, and lists that will help you assess your work needs and goals. You can also access all of the tools in the chapter at KristinMeekhof.com.

chapter eight

the best advice i never got

things widows know

Don't lean on others. Accept love and understanding, but don't make anyone—especially your children—feel that they can't get on with their own lives. At first I was talking to my kids too much about what I was feeling, but I realized this wasn't fair to them, and I stopped.

—MARCY, 61

I would strongly recommend that any widow wait a few years and get counseling before she remarries. I was comparing every man to my husband. It was obvious to me after a while that I was thinking of my husband all the time; to me that meant it was too early to be thinking of getting married again.

—MELISSA, 57

IN THIS CHAPTER, WE'LL EXPLORE MANY OF THE THINGS widows learn and wish someone had told them ahead of time. To start, I (Jim) want to share an eye-opening experience I had with one of the widows I interviewed over the phone for the book, a fifty-seven-year-old woman named Lynn.

When I explained the idea of the book and the kinds of questions we were asking, Lynn went into a tirade.

"First of all, I resent you calling me a widow," Lynn said in a strident voice. "You and everyone else want to tell me who I am. So you use the term 'widow.' I am not a widow. I'm me! I was married to Jerry; now I'm not. But when you call me a widow, you are not willing to discover me. What you're doing is conveniently putting a label on me as a person who suffered a loss. And it implies that I am a damaged person because of my loss. I'm more than that, so don't call me a widow!"

Initially, I felt like Lynn was attacking me. It felt personal. The interview, however, switched gears soon and we spent forty-five minutes talking about her loss and how she dealt with it. I didn't even use the term "widow" after her initial reaction. When the interview ended, I went for a long bike ride as I tried to process what Lynn had said. I concluded that she was angry with me and anyone else who would see her only as a woman who lost a husband, and I got that.

As Kristin and I did dozens more interviews alone and together over the next year, no one else responded quite like Lynn had. But every so often I would think of Lynn. There was always the nagging thought she was telling me something I didn't quite understand. Maybe I couldn't understand. Her reaction had gotten me thinking, and I started to wonder if other widows felt the same way as Lynn but perhaps were hiding it. It concerned me that this might be an important message we hadn't addressed in the book so far.

A year later, Vicki Lind, a career counselor, mentioned in a conversation that she thought the work of William Bridges was important for her work with widows. So I began reading his books on transitions and communicated with his widow, Susan. Transitions, Bridges wrote in several books, such as *Managing Transitions* and *Transitions: Making Sense of Life's Changes*, force us to forge a new identity. But to emerge from a life change with a new identity means giving up the old identity, which can be indescribably hard. And that's when I remembered talking to Lynn.

For most of her life, Lynn, like most widows, had an identity as a married woman and as one half of a couple. It was Jerry and Lynn. She was Jerry's wife. But who was she after Jerry died? Was she, indeed, Jerry's widow? Or Lynn the widow? Or someone else?

And that's what Lynn was angry about. She recognized on some level that she couldn't live out the rest of her life as Jerry's widow, nor did she want to. That didn't allow her to construct a new identity. To come up with a new identity, she would have to give up the old one. She would have to be a new Lynn who wasn't connected with Jerry.

Bridges wrote that this is not easy to do. In fact, he said, it is very uncomfortable. Giving up who we have learned to be is unsettling. But widows, if they want a new identity, must give up the older, more comfortable one as wife. As we wrote in Chapter One, there is an initial period of disorientation when your spouse dies. You suddenly don't know who you are. It may take two or three years to begin to forge the new identity. William Bridges would say that your spouse dying is the change; you becoming a person separate from any association with your partner involves a transition and a transformation.

This is what many widows know. But not many can truly articulate it. Nor are many of them as angry about the transition or resentful of the struggle that it involves as was Lynn—at least on that day. What we can take away from this is that every woman who loses a spouse must forge a new identity. But doing that means giving up your former identity. That takes time, patience, and courage. What we found was that after many years, most widows were, in fact, doing this.

BUT WIDOWS KNOW MANY OTHER THINGS TOO!

Here is what Kristin says: As a widow myself, I learned a great deal after Roy died. I've shared some of that in previous chapters. I will share more of the insights I learned along this journey toward successfully coping with my grief. However, the many widows we interviewed were so forthcoming in telling us about their journeys that it gave us much to think about—often this information was volunteered and not in response to our questions. It was evident when we started talking to women who had lost a spouse that we needed a special chapter to communicate the many valuable things they had learned and what they knew. So this chapter is a forum to pass on their collected wisdom.

This chapter, therefore, includes firsthand advice from widows about marriage, dating, sex, working with hospice, health, caregiving, regret, healing, evolving, and more. Some of the comments are from widows who were in very flawed marriages. Their observations will provide solace for the reader who has lost a spouse who was far from perfect, had substance abuse problems, or was abusive or unfaithful. Other widows had happy marriages and share comments that are particularly insightful about how to heal and create a happy and hopeful future.

FACING RESIDUAL ISSUES FROM YOUR MARRIAGE AFTER LOSS

Marriage may seem like the proverbial bed of roses at first. There is the blush of a new romance and the thrill of two people being deeply in love. However, there are no roses without thorns. And that marital bliss that seems so perfect in the beginning may—as the years go on—not be so blissful after all. What seems so perfect in the first few months and even years can turn out to be far less idyllic than you thought.

That's what Julie Metz, author of *Perfection*, discovered. Within days of her husband Henry's death, Julie's friend Emily and her husband found emails between Henry and another woman. In an attempt to shelter Julie from the pain, Emily and her husband deleted the emails. Later, Emily revealed the other woman's name when Julie asked. Julie writes in *Perfection* that "seven months earlier Henry's death had been a random medical catastrophe, a tragedy that had caused so much misery for Liza [their child] and me. Hundreds of sad people [were] at his funeral. Now it looked more like the great escape."

Some time later, as she reflected back on his many affairs, she wrote: "I couldn't kill Henry anymore, since he was, conveniently enough, dead."

Anger is not uncommon for widows, but it comes in many different forms. Some widows may indeed be angry because of the unfairness of death stealing their spouse or the fact that a tragedy has ended their otherwise happy relationship. Other women are angry after their partner's death about other thorns that commonly affect marriages—affairs (as in Julie Metz's case), substance abuse, an absence of physical affection, poor communication, physical abuse, money issues, and suicide (if that was the cause of the partner's death). These things can destroy a marriage while both partners are alive, and in death they can create deep pockets of lasting pain for widows. Carol Staudacher writes in *A Time to Grieve* that "to have an intimate relationship with anyone means knowing that person's faults and weaknesses as well as his or her strengths and virtues. In death, as in life, we recognize both and accept both."

That's easily said but not so easily achieved, which was revealed to us when talking to widows. While some, like Katherine—whose husband committed suicide and cut short a marriage she thought was very satisfying—can say they truly have no malice toward their husbands, other widows recall bitter fights, patterns of infidelity, and missed opportunities. Still others were on their way to divorce court when their husbands died.

Mary Beth explained that at the time of her husband's death, they were separated due to his addiction to painkillers. "I thought that getting me and our child away from him would give him the motivation he needed to enter recovery," Mary Beth told us. But it didn't. Instead, he went on using a variety of prescription medications, which led to a heart attack and his almost immediate death—leaving her as a single parent to a young child.

Other widows discover infidelity after the death. For example, Ruth Anne, after a forty-year marriage, was widowed at age sixty-eight. While going through several boxes in the attic that her husband had left behind, she discovered love letters written while he was serving in the military just after Ruth Anne and he were married.

"They were highly suggestive letters," Ruth Anne said, "and one even included a proposal for marriage—even though we were already married."

For years after finding the letters, Ruth Anne was devastated by thoughts of his unfaithfulness and she constantly tried to push aside her angry and hurt emotions. When she couldn't successfully avoid thinking about it, she went to see a therapist. Only after acknowledging those feelings and accepting her emotions was she able to regain a balance in her life. "I could finally accept his failings," Ruth Anne said, "and I could see that whatever he had done, his positive qualities far outweighed the secret I had uncovered."

Julie Metz had a sixteen-year relationship with her husband and a six-and-a-half-year-old daughter when he died suddenly from a pulmonary embolism. She was forty-three at the time, but after his death, she soon discovered he had had five affairs, including one with her closest friend, a woman who had sobbed uncontrollably at the funeral.

"Friends and family returned to their lives, the house was quiet. My new loneliness frightened me. Living alone with my child was not what I had planned," she wrote. But, after uncovering the affairs, her friends attempted to console her with some comforting words. "'He loved you so much. He always said so. I don't understand,' said one bewildered friend after another. Their confusion was comfort. I felt less like a complete idiot, but only slightly less. Mostly, I felt like I'd been hit by a truck," Julie wrote.

As devastating as this can be—recognizing that the man you loved betrayed you—you, like Julie and Ruth Anne, can move on. It may take some sessions with a therapist to put things into perspective, but whether you get help or do it on your own, it is all about coming to grips with your own emotions and then seeing your situation in a new light. Ultimately, women who have overcome anger and betrayal have been able to release that their spouses' actions said less about them as wives than it said about their spouses and their flaws and demons.

RUMINATING ON YOUR REGRETS

Other widows may replay sections of their marriages over and over again, resulting in sleepless nights and tremendous emotional turmoil. Earl Grollman warns against this process in his book *Living When a Loved One Has Died*. Grollman says that "self-recrimination becomes a way to undo all the things that make you now feel guilty." Any widows who are critical of their past actions and regularly listen to the inner voice that asserts, "You should have done this or that" sets up an inner cycle of melodrama that is very difficult to break, and struggling with the guilt this creates can be extremely taxing.

This kind of critical self-talk is not uncommon for widows—or indeed for anyone, married or not—but it can be far more intense if your spouse's death was related to substance abuse, depression, or suicide. Indeed, reliving your emotional issues related to this particular kind of loss is incredibly painful. For example, you may blame others, including your spouse, as you think about the less-than-perfect past of your marriage. When the death is related to substance abuse or suicide, you may want to manipulate past memories and events to make it easier to tell others about the death.

Katherine, whose husband died by hanging himself one morning in their bedroom while she was at work, said she made up stories to tell others about his death.

"Initially I would lie and say my husband had a heart attack," Katherine said. "Then, I would say he died of a broken heart. For a while I told people he was sick and depressed. Eventually, I got to the point when I could just come out and tell people my husband killed himself."

When you have to lie about your husband and his death, what you are trying to do is soothe yourself and take some of the sting out of the reality. Author and speaker Marianne Williamson says in *The Gift of Change*, "So often we try to hide who we are rather than heal who we are." Taking an honest inventory of your true self, including the circumstances of your marriage and the kind of person your spouse was, will lead to healing.

In the meantime, though, it is not unusual to ruminate by continually reflecting on past memories, thinking about what you did, what he did, and what either of you could have done differently. This is totally normal, but it's important to address these ruminations head on so you can release the pain through forgiveness. Otherwise, you may develop a raw emotional wound inside you that will prevent you from healing and creating a new future for yourself. You may even become overly sensitive to any issue related to your pain and find yourself pushing others away.

For example, if your spouse was critical about your appearance and implied you had gained weight since your wedding day, you might develop an open sore related to your appearance. Then, if someone at work mentions a new diet or asks you to walk regularly during your lunch hour, the sore is rubbed again. You immediately assume they think you are fat and that you need to go on a diet or get more exercise, even though they never said that. This is because you associate such comments with your spouse. So whenever someone mentions weight-related topics, you withdraw instead of realizing your coworker is more likely concerned about their own weight or health—none of which has anything to do with you.

DEVELOPING SELF-COMPASSION

Another way to soften your inner critic is to develop self-compassion. Kristin Neff's book *Self-Compassion* is all about being compassionate toward your own failings and imperfections, which can bring about greater well-being than when you repeatedly judge yourself. This is not to be confused with being narcissistic or having an inflated sense of self-worth. Instead it means being gentle with yourself. Neff says that "by giving ourselves unconditional kindness and comfort while embracing the human experience, difficult as it is, we avoid destructive patterns of fear, negativity, and isolation."

Nothing is more difficult than feeling isolated and alone with negative memories of your marriage. Being hard on yourself by constantly piling on more blame, feeling more anger, and striving to be more perfect will only create more anxiety. In *The Places That Scare You*, American Buddhist nun and author Pema Chödrön offers this view on compassion toward oneself: "When we practice generating compassion, we can expect to experience the fear of our pain. Compassion practice is daring. It involves learning to relax and allow ourselves to move gently toward what scares us."

In another book called *When Things Fall Apart*, Chodron says this: "What we hate in ourselves, we'll hate in others. To the degree that we have compassion for ourselves, we will also have compassion for others. Having compassion starts and ends with having compassion for all those unwanted parts of ourselves, for all those imperfections that we don't even want to look at."

Being fearful of people finding out that your spouse was hooked on heroin, drank a fifth of vodka every day, or committed suicide complicates your grief. It is painful to even think about your spouse drinking himself to death or dying due to an overdose of sleeping pills or shooting himself in the head, let alone accept that he was in so much emotional and psychological pain that he ended his life in such a horrible way. Debra Holland says in *The Essential Guide to Grief and Grieving*, "While it's difficult to believe for those who haven't experienced it, suicidal individuals are in deep (perhaps secret) pain and depression. They can have twisted and unrealistic thinking. They think their suffering will never end. They don't understand the damage they will do to loved ones because they believe family and friends are better off without them. They can't see any other solution to their problems. To them, it's the only answer."

WHAT WIDOWS SAID

There is no workbook or rules on this. We don't have to know the answers to everything. But be patient with yourself. If there ever was a time to be weak, it is now! If you need to be weak and vulnerable, then so be it. Just take care of you.

—CECI, 29

DEPRESSION AND SUICIDE

Deep clinical depression can involve distorted thinking. If you are very depressed, you are unable to view the world in a realistic, clear way. For example, if you wear prescription glasses, you know how difficult it is to see clearly without them. The world and the people in it—even your own family—are fuzzy. You see shadows, and depending on the severity of your vision, you may have trouble figuring out what the images are. Clinical depression involving thoughts of suicide can be similar. All of us may be depressed at times as a result of what others might see as minor, insignificant problems. A transient, short-lived depression will not blur your vision much. But for someone who has been suffering from depression for a long time, it is like being legally blind and trying to function without your thick glasses. Depression, like poor vision, can involve varying degrees of perception. A seriously depressed individual may not be able to see any reasonable or practical solutions to their problems. They often reject help from others—even a beloved spouse. As a result, they may feel isolated. No matter what the reality is, this is their perception.

Sometimes mental health issues in a family have been kept secret, so you may not know the entire family history. Katherine, however, knew her husband found his own mother's body after she killed herself. That happened when he was a boy. Katherine didn't know—and probably will never know—however, how much of a role this played in her husband's suicide. But other widows didn't find out until much later that there was suicide, clinical depression, or serious addictions in their spouses' families. Even if you knew everything about your spouse's family history, you still may not have been able to help him, prevent his death, or even have a better understanding of how his death came about.

WHAT WIDOWS SAID

His suicide is a part of my life, but it's not who I am. I'm not Arthur's suicide.

—TINA, 54

Widows of suicide victims told us there were no obvious signs prior to a suicide. Women told us the days or hours leading up to it were pleasant—not at all filled with tension and agitation. While we cannot judge or determine exactly what happened with your spouse, we at least can offer a perspective. Many depressed individuals have determined well in advance that they are going to commit suicide. Perhaps they wanted the control over the manner of their death or the time of their death. Nothing you could have said or done would have stopped their suicide. No matter the timing or means of their death, in their mind, they may have done what they could—given their impaired perception—to save you from painful memories. Some choose to kill themselves after a peaceful or happy evening. Sometimes the suicide occurs when it looks like there is every reason to be optimistic about the future.

Still you wonder, "Well, if everything is going fine, then why did they do it?" The perspective we offer is that your spouse may have chosen to have a peaceful last conversation with you, so that the last verbal exchange you had was not in anger.

Understanding Suicide

According to the *Morbidity and Mortality Weekly Report*, it used to be that the number of people who died in automobile crashes in the United States far outranked other causes of death. But that's changed in recent years. The Centers for Disease Control and Prevention (CDC) reports that as of 2009, suicides have surpassed fatalities from automobile accidents. In 2010, there were about 38,000 suicides compared to about 35,000 deaths related to car accidents. And the people who are now killing themselves more often? It's middle-aged adults between the ages of 35 and 64. The suicide rate for people in this age range rose to 17.6 per 100,000 people in 2010 from 13.7 per 100,000 in 1999, an increase of almost 30 percent.

The CDC suggests that the increase in suicides among the middle-aged might be due to the economic downturn of the past several years and an increase in drug abuse among adults. Although there were increases in the number of suicides by firearms and poison, the biggest increase was in suffocation—mostly due to hanging.

Suicide is currently listed as the eleventh leading cause of death in the United States. With 38,000 people committing suicide each year, that works out to be 104 people a day, or about one every fourteen minutes. Given these statistics, it is very likely that you know of someone who killed themselves—or you lost someone this way.

Death by suicide often creates shame, and you may feel compelled to defend your spouse—indeed your whole family. Of course, this doesn't mean that you need to send out a mass email explaining the personal details of his struggles, but being completely honest and compassionate with yourself is a critical step toward healing. It is necessary to give yourself grace. This is the same grace you would extend to your closest friend. It does not come with judgment but through forgiveness. Forgive yourself and eventually your spouse. If you can't forgive your spouse, start with yourself. In *Living When a Loved One Has Died,* Rabbi Earl Grollman added this about self-forgiveness: "A wise member of the clergy once said, 'I believe that God forgives you. The question is: Will you forgive yourself?'"

WHAT WIDOWS SAID

You never stop loving your spouse after they die. You never stop missing them. It just feels less intensely painful over time. I don't remember anyone telling me that it would physically hurt as much as it did at the beginning. I also didn't think that I would not only mourn the present loss of my husband but also mourn all our future plans that were spoken and unspoken.

—ANNE MARIE, 51

Dismantling the stories behind the suicide death or accidental overdose death of a spouse can be scary for a widow, but often it is part of the healing process. In our experience, widows often want to share the stories of their spouse's death—not just their spouse's symptoms of depression. A support group specific to suicide or substance abuse can provide widows this type of support. Within a support group, you can find communal pain, in that your grief story—along with those of others—will share a common thread of unresolved pain and sorrow. A group can offer you the opportunity to share your story without fear of others passing judgment. Although this will not change the way your story ends, being able to share your entire narrative with others who have experienced the same thing provides a measure of comfort.

Handling Your Own Depression

Clinical depression is often a medical issue. If you are thinking about suicide now because you are so devastated about the loss of your spouse, you need to seek immediate psychiatric care. You need to be completely honest with the professionals to get the correct services. Do not try to minimize your thoughts or feelings because you are ashamed. You need to explain that your spouse died, you feel that your entire life is over, and you are having trouble coping with the loss.

Pauline Laurent, who was widowed at age twenty-two when she was seven months pregnant, knows about the repercussions of denied grief.

"After twenty-five years of living in denial," Pauline recalls, "I was writing suicide notes to my daughter. I was two hundred pounds and was diagnosed with a clinical depression. I was using excessive amounts of food to numb myself and avoid facing the grief."

Pauline says that by the grace of God, she didn't commit suicide. "When I turned around and faced my grief," she says, "a Higher Intelligence met me and carried me through to the other side. I found teachers along the way who could help. Seeing a therapist weekly, writing about my loss, and Buddhist meditation were the things that allowed me to finally face myself. Before then, I was always 'busy,' running away from the grief, trying to stay ahead of it—but I could never do that."

After her husband's death in 1968, Pauline returned to college and obtained a bachelor of science in education. In later years, she was trained and certified as a certified professional co-active coach (CPCC) through the Coaches Training Institute. Her story of reconciliation is beautifully written in her memoir, *Grief Denied: A Vietnam Widow's Story*. Since becoming a coach, she has worked with thousands of people to further their personal and professional development.

Pauline advises widows and others to think of grief as an energy that follows you around. "If you have a significant loss and you don't deal with it," she cautions, "the grief follows you. Then you have another loss and another loss—and the grief keeps chasing you."

The repercussions of denied grief are anger or chronic depression that saps the life force from us, or it can attack our bodies and make us physically sick. Joy and sorrow are linked, and when we don't process grief, our ability to experience joy is hampered. And without moments of joy, life seems hardly worth the effort. Here are her suggestions about how to face your grief:

* Meet weekly with a professional who has done her grief work so she can witness yours. Work with her for as long as it takes.
* Schedule some down time in your day to avoid being too busy.
* Start writing or find a creative way to express your feelings.
* Do whatever allows and encourages you to go inward and get in touch with the deeper feelings around your loss.
* Avoid people who can't witness your grief and may subtly encourage you get over it and get on with it.
* Join a twelve-step recovery group if you are using a substance such as alcohol, drugs, or food to numb your pain.

COMING TO TERMS WITH YOUR SPOUSE'S SUBSTANCE ABUSE

If your spouse was a substance abuser—whether that substance was alcohol, an illegal drug, or prescription medicines—you will have to cope with the disappointment, and perhaps anger, you may feel about his death. Samantha is an example of how marriage to a substance abuser can change your life. And the feelings you have about his substance abuse won't end with his death.

"At first I didn't even want to tell you about my full story," Samantha confided in an interview. "We were divorced for a short while before he died. I didn't want you to know about this, because I didn't know how you would feel about me. Although I feel bad, I need to tell you the whole story.

"Jim was my high school sweetheart. We met when we were both seventeen. He never smoked, didn't do drugs, and he was a football player. He was a great guy. He hung out with a bunch of guys at the gym, but that's where he started taking steroids. That gave him mood swings."

Samantha went on to reveal that after they were married, Jim and his friends began taking sedatives, muscle relaxers, and Vicodin. "He did these drugs for many years, and I did all I could to help him. But I finally decided I had to get me and my daughter away from him, so I had to divorce him. Being married to him was frustrating and exhausting. It was hard for me watching him go downhill, and even more upsetting that I couldn't help him."

When Jim was thirty-four, it all caught up with him and he died of a sudden heart attack. Their daughter was ten years old. "Although it was hard living with him and trying to help him, it was even more upsetting to see my daughter grow up without a dad," Samantha said.

A consolation is that her daughter has done so well. "She did well in school and was involved in many antidrug campaigns," Samantha said. "She has become a huge role model to other teens. I am so proud of her."

Samantha added at the end of the interview that just talking about this still makes her cry. "I loved him a lot and know he loved us," Samantha said. "I wish things were different. But life goes on. The worst part is that I talked to him on the day he died. He cried on the phone, telling me he was going to get off of all the drugs."

Living with a substance abuser can be as just as frustrating as Samantha's story suggests. He may have made many promises to quit and to clean up his life. He may have had every intention of changing, but after hearing these so often, you may have felt—like Samantha—that you had no choice but to give up and get away. And like Samantha, you may have done everything in your power to help him get clean and sober—all without success. And therein lies the ultimate—and lasting—frustration and guilt that comes from being with a drug abuser or an alcoholic: maybe there was something else you could have done or said that would have made a difference. And, as we will advise, that's where forgiveness comes in.

WHAT WIDOWS SAID

My loss is complicated because he was my ex-husband and we had a tumultuous marriage. He was very verbally abusive toward me, and then after we got divorced when my son was thirteen, there was this exhausting custody battle. Our son was torn between us and also in the middle of all of this. I got remarried within a couple of years, but my first husband never got over my remarriage and did everything he could to make my life miserable. About a year ago, he was shot and killed in a hunting accident. And I've had to grieve for a man who caused me so much pain.

—STACY, 43

MANAGING REGRETS FROM SEPARATION OR DIVORCE

Marriage problems, separation, or even divorce may have preceded your spouse's death. Maybe the marital problems developed out of his substance abuse, although, of course, marriages can suffer for many other reasons. But if there were marriage problems or a divorce, then, like Stacy, you may have various experiences you didn't anticipate.

For instance, if you were remarried, like some widows we talked to, going to your first spouse's funeral may be uncomfortable. Or you may feel like an outcast there. That will be particularly true if he was remarried. In effect, there is no role for the ex-wife at a funeral. In fact, you may endure outright hostility from his family or friends.

Given your present relationships or life circumstances, you may not have the appropriate time and space to properly grieve this loss. Although you might have imagined before his death that your pain or even guilt for divorcing him would eventually end, with his death, you may realize that there is no particular redemption from the pain.

Healing from grief and loss doesn't come easily or in one fell swoop. It is frequently slow, gradual, and more painful than you thought it would be.

Stacy told us that after her husband's death, she remembered lots of good times they had, although she could never totally forget the memories of abuse and his torment of her. It is not uncommon for an old memory that once again makes you feel sad, vulnerable, or guilty to be jogged by a conversation or even a photograph.

Kristin, three years after her husband died, remembers finding a Valentine's Day card between the pages of a book. "It brought me to tears," she said. "Right then, everything for me stopped. That valentine brought back memories. I remember we disagreed about how long we were going to stay in Florida that year the card was given to me. Now in retrospect, it was a trivial discussion; it wasn't a heated argument, but I still cringe thinking I was snippy and unkind."

Carol Lee, 39, a year following her husband's death from a heart attack, can talk about the regret she feels because of her own behavior. "Cal and I were different," she says. "He was a free spirit, and I was the cautious, practical one. He'd want to go on vacations or trips and I would say that I couldn't because of my job. I know now I worked a lot and put my job ahead of him sometimes."

FORGIVING YOUR HUSBAND AND YOURSELF

Forgiveness can be excruciating and exhausting under normal circumstances, but in the wake of death, it can be most painful. You may feel that you don't have it in you to forgive how he may have hurt you. But forgiveness may be necessary for your optimal psychological well-being. Forgiveness of your spouse for any or all of his shortcomings and failures will diminish your fears and other emotions and will lead to healing.

Rabbi Shneur Zalman explains that it is possible to heal despite being broken. "A broken heart is not the same as sadness," Rabbi Zalman says. "Sadness occurs when the heart is stone-cold and lifeless. On the contrary, there is an unbelievable amount of vitality in a broken heart." When you see someone on the news forgiving the person who killed their child in a drunk-driving accident and wonder how this is possible, this is the vitality that Rabbi Zalman is speaking about.

Others create foundations in their spouses' names. You may not be in such a dramatic situation as this, but self-compassion, authenticity, and forgiveness are born from this vitality.

Years after Roy died, I wondered what clues I could have missed that he had stage four asymptomatic adrenal cancer. Without truly understanding the stages of adrenal cancer, I could not comprehend how one could be so near death. I met with an adrenal cancer specialist at the hospital that treated Roy. He spoke with me for an hour about the progression of the disease. This shattered my logic, that a progressive cancer can be asymptomatic. Sensing my guilt, he finally said, "There was nothing else that you could have done."

This may be natural to wonder; however, it also shows a fracture still present in the grief process. In writing this now, I can't say that I have completely forgiven myself. The conversation with the doctor did help. The guilt about the cancer doesn't devour me as it once did. The brokenness isn't as great. But self-forgiveness didn't come all at once. Small things can still make me think about this time. Does this mean that I haven't completely forgiven myself? Perhaps, but I have made progress, and when I look back at that time, it is less painful to recall. So I think this means, in some small way, that I have forgiven myself.

Depending on the circumstances surrounding your spouse's death, forgiveness may come in small increments. Problems develop when we expect too much from ourselves. We think we shouldn't lament. We shouldn't dwell on the past. It is natural to rethink what happened. To ask ourselves, "Why?" We may never get the answers we seek, and this is where the challenge lies. How do we go on to find healing when we feel deserted by our loved ones? I contend that for many widows, it is a process, and if you are expecting an aha moment in which complete forgiveness suddenly appears, you are sure to be disappointed. There's nothing wrong with you if it takes years to finally give up all guilt and discover you no longer need to find forgiveness.

In talking with the widows for this book, I learned that each went about the healing process a little differently, but nearly all widows had unresolved questions and nearly all widows experienced some level of guilt. This was especially true if they had been caregivers—most of us widows have!—for any length of time while their spouse was dying. Many of the widows I got to know found healing in doing something for others. It is ironic that they acquired guilt by caring for their husbands and not being able to stop them from dying, but they were able, in altruistic actions, by doing something good and kind for others, to lessen their guilt.

ADVICE FOR CAREGIVERS

Becoming a widow may not have been easy. While Roy's illness was not especially easy for either Roy or Kristin, it was mercifully of short duration. For others, the caregiving period may have been lengthy. Such was the case with Jill Gafner.

Jill, who is now fifty-six and the author of *Personal Positioning for the Caregiver*, was only thirty-two when her husband was diagnosed with lung cancer. Soon after that, they both found out he had brain cancer. Doctors said he had a few short weeks to live. But Bob Gafner lived for twenty-one years, during which time Jill had to work full-time to support the family, becoming not only the primary caregiver but the primary income provider for a family of five.

During those years, she learned a lot about the role of the caregiver. For one thing, "Nobody cares for the caregiver," she said recently. And she went on to say that along with the plight of the caregiver being overlooked, there is avoidance by friends and family. "My friends went away," Jill says simply. "Not because they didn't care; it was because they knew I had a full plate. Inviting me out to a social event wouldn't cross their minds since it would appear insensitive to my stretched agenda.

"To justify distance in relationships, our friends typically think, *If she needs me I told her to call me—she hasn't called me, she must be doing all right.*" And often nothing could be further from the truth, says Gafner.

She adds, "If I had had one person say to me, 'I know what you're going through,' it would have been wonderful."

But nobody says that to the caregiver. There is sympathy for the sick and dying spouse, but—unless you've been there—no one really understands what it is like for the person providing care.

Jill recalls what she was feeling during those years while she felt like she had two full-time jobs, that of an office worker and that of a caregiver: "I was lost, lonely, guilty, sad, and angry." Some of those feelings, Jill explains, are related to your inability to make your spouse well or to keep him from dying.

Jill took what she learned as a caregiver and turned it into a way to help others by writing about her experiences and speaking before audiences. "There are more than fifty million people in this country providing care for others," she said in a presentation to caregivers recently. "Many of those caregivers will die before their patients due to the stress associated with caregiving." And, she points out, 67 percent of caregivers in this country are women.

WHAT WIDOWS SAID

My advice to other women is if your husband has Alzheimer's, don't use medication to prolong his life—it isn't worth it.

—ARLENE, 72

Jill has advice for women who are still caregivers for a seriously ill husband: "Your friends are waiting for you to call them, so call them. Let them know you need their help."

And whether you are still giving care or that phase of your life has passed, Jill suggests that each day you wake up your mind, your body, and your soul. "It's a matter of your own survival and sometimes you have to think of something other than your patient," she says.

HOSPICE

My husband died in our home about a week after we began hospice. It was only about three weeks before he died that we were told his cancer was terminal. Before that point, it wasn't clear that the cancer wasn't treatable. Almost immediately upon hearing this terrible news, Roy surrendered to his prognosis. This didn't mean that he gave up, but he wasn't in denial either. Instead, Roy befriended death in a way. He held a deep faith in God and firmly believed that he would go to heaven. He thought that accepting death would make it easier on me as well. Roy knew how and where he wanted to die; he wanted to use hospice and die at home.

Hospice has been a concept of caring derived from medieval times, where it developed as a place where travelers and the sick, wounded, or dying could find rest and comfort. While the origins of hospice can be traced back to the eleventh century, it was in the late nineteenth century and the twentieth century in Britain and the United States that hospice care expanded and become a vital part of the health-care system. Contemporary hospice organizations offer a comprehensive program of care to patients and families facing a life-threatening illness. Hospice is primarily a concept of care, not a specific place of care, although in the United States it often occurs at home.

Hospice emphasizes palliative rather than curative treatment. That is, it prioritizes the quality at the end of an individual's life over efforts to prolong the life of a terminally ill patient. The patient and family are included in the care plan and emotional, spiritual, and practical support is given based on the patient's wishes and the family's needs. Most important, the dying person is comforted and sophisticated symptom relief is provided. Trained volunteers offer respite care for family members as well as meaningful support to the patient.

During the last days of Roy's life, I was the primary caregiver. I have to admit that I didn't care for the hospice staff. I sought out the help of a dear friend who had cared for hospice patients. Within a few days, on my own, I was changing the sheets of Roy's bed while he occupied it, administering morphine, helping him to the bathroom, eventually changing his diaper, bathing him while in bed, and taking copious notes about status. I learned how to carefully turn his body so that he would not develop bed sores, something I feared. No one ever actually asked to review my scribbled notes, but I was deeply afraid that if I didn't do everything medically right, someone would remove Roy from my care.

But I also felt that hospice was the last gift I could give Roy, and this in some small way made me grateful for it. The days of hospice were filled with sorrow. In essence, I was watching his organs slowly shut down and his body weaken to the point that he eventually slipped into a coma.

In hindsight, I should have asked for more help. Little in my life before Roy's illness prepared me for this end-of-life scenario. Providing hospice in our home was overwhelming and painful. Yet it is still something I look at as a gift.

DATING, SEX, AND REMARRIAGE

While you may not be emotionally ready to even begin thinking about dating or a new relationship for a year or two—or even longer—after your spouse dies, remember if you have been that caregiver who was looking after an ill spouse with a fatal diagnosis, you may have started grieving long before he died. To people on the outside of your personal experience—even your children—it may look like it is too soon after your husband's death to start a relationship. However, if you have been caring for him and watching him fade away, you may be quite ready to move on into other relationships.

One widow, who was just past forty when her husband died, told us about beginning a new relationship less than a year after his death.

"I met Justin about nine months after my husband passed on," Francine told us. "He was a beautiful young man."

She said that she wasn't looking for a relationship, certainly not a sexual relationship at that point in her life. "But I didn't say no to opportunity either. I was safe from hurt because my true relationship was still with Bill, albeit a ghost. This lovely fellow held me as I cried and made me feel good after feeling so, so bad for so long."

Both Francine and Barbara engaged in sexual relationships, which for both were temporary but healing in a way as well. Neither was ready for a long-term relationship—certainly not with a much younger man. Nonetheless, a sexual relationship served as a bridge as they moved along in their grief. There is nothing wrong with this. If you are in a sexual relationship you know is temporary but you feel is helping you heal, that's great. If you aren't ready for that yet, there's nothing wrong with waiting until you feel ready as well. The important thing is to go with what feels right for you.

Remarriage

Like so many widows we talked to who felt they were still in the prime of their lives, you may hope that someone comes along that you can love and share the rest of your life with. While Francine met a young man with whom she could have a brief affair, most of the women we interviewed very strongly recommended one thing: "You should wait a few years and get counseling before you remarry," was the way one widow put it.

Nothing is more of a hot button topic than widows and dating or, to put it frankly, widows and sex. One widow, Nina, said that she and her late husband had infrequent sex. After he died, she felt free to have sex with other men, but she still missed her husband. For Nina, dating brought mixed emotions.

Although most widows will consider dating or remarriage at some point, for many there are roadblocks to just going out and starting to date. One barrier is their feelings that they are being disloyal to their late spouses by thinking about being with someone else. The other is much more practical: meeting someone you would like to be with.

Of course, the traditional ways of meeting people—friends, religious communities, and social organizations or events—are still options. However, these days more and more people use the Internet to find someone to date.

According to the Pew Research Center, one in ten Americans has used an online dating site or mobile dating app themselves, and many more people now know someone else who uses online dating or who has found a spouse or long-term partner through online dating. In general, public attitudes toward online dating have become much more positive in recent years. Social networking sites such as Match .com, eHarmony, and OkCupid now play a prominent role when it comes to navigating and documenting romantic relationships. The Pew Research Center's studies estimates that 38 percent of Americans who are single and actively looking for a partner have used online dating at one point or another. And 66 percent of online daters have gone on a date with someone they met through a dating site or app, with 23 percent of online daters reporting that they have met a spouse or developed a long-term relationship through these sites.

Our advice to you is to proceed with caution when it comes to dating, especially online dating. One advantage of being introduced to someone through mutual friends is that your friend is able to provide a bit of history about your date's background. Unfortunately, some widows are emotionally and financially vulnerable. This vulnerability and fragility combined with a need for companionship can sometimes lead to poor choices. It is natural to want to seek someone out you can date, but be very clear with yourself about your intentions. Here are some questions to ask yourself:

* Would you have dated this person at any other time of your life?
* What would your spouse think about your new friend?
* Have you introduced your new friend to others?

- What is their opinion of him?
- Are you seeking out someone around the anniversary of your spouse's death, your spouse's birthday, or your marital anniversary?
- When you leave the date, how do you feel about this person?
- Why do you want to date someone at this time?

We know that grief can create a blind spot and it may be tricky to clearly see the real person you are dating. Usually family and close friends—for better or worse—will tell you what they think about the person you are dating, so don't be afraid to consult them for feedback. Also, be aware most people need a period of time after a traumatic event in their life. That period is a minimum of about two years for most of us. While casual dating may be fine during this readjustment period when you are learning to live with the loss of your spouse, jumping into a relationship may be fraught with dangers. Some widows have told us that they were still thinking about and talking about their spouses—which naturally drove the new romantic interest away, since it was clear that she had not resolved her feelings toward her spouse or come to terms with the loss. All of this is why we're telling you to be careful when you approach dating, though we're not trying to dissuade you from dating at all!

CHILDREN AND REMARRIAGE

As mental health professionals, we strongly recommend that you seek the guidance of a trusted professional if you have children from a previous marriage and plan to remarry. We all have blind spots for our own situations, and a professional can offer you a different perspective about your family dynamics. This is not to say that you are doing something reckless, but it is important to take your children's developmental and emotional needs into consideration. Often children wonder what role their new father figure will have in their daily life. And for children, actions speak louder than words. Children will notice, for instance, that their father's photographs are no longer present in the home or that they have been moved to a less visible spot. They will also pick up on it if talk about their father is discouraged.

Just because your children are not talking to you about their father doesn't mean they are not thinking about him. I know about some of this because I was nearly five when my father died and my mother and I were all alone. She was alone in her grief and I was lonely without the one central person in my life that I could relate to. But about a year after my father died, my mother started dating. And it was a year after that that she announced she would be getting remarried. She added that my father would want this for both of us. I was seven at this time, and it is with childlike innocence that I took her words to heart and truly thought that this would be the end to my sadness.

I was in her wedding as a flower girl. I fully supported my mother and even went along with changing my last name. Her husband said that he would legally adopt me and we would become a new family. I would call him "Dad." My last name, it seemed to me, was the only connection I had to my late father, but I accepted the name change— something I regret to this day.

Now I recognize that my mother's remarriage was important to her, and I fully appreciate that it was a successful marriage for her. And I have talked to many widows who, like my mother, got a second chance at happiness with a second marriage. But try to see things from your children's point of view and what it might mean to them. If you have older children, go to the section in Chapter Six called "Getting Remarried or Finding a Domestic Partner" to learn about some of the financial implications of remarriage.

DEALING WITH THE ANNIVERSARY OF HIS DEATH

What do you do around the anniversary date of his death?

What can be most disappointing for many widows is that no one seems to remember the anniversary of your spouse's death, so you may experience some fresh symptoms of grief all over again. There is nothing wrong with that. In fact, being aware of and proactive about how you approach this anniversary is very important for your own emotional health. If possible, try not to schedule major events, such as a move or an important work project, around the anniversary because you may feel very distracted and unmotivated. Or share with a friend that you are anticipating a difficult week and ask for their support. You could suggest sharing a meal together on the day itself because the distraction may be what you need for even just a few hours. Or schedule a phone call or visit with family members, children, or even in-laws (if you are close with them) for the day or week of the anniversary. Sometimes sharing memories or just connecting with others who knew your partner on the anniversary of his death can help ease the pain a bit.

One woman we talked to said, "I notice about a week prior to the anniversary of Sid's death that my subconscious mind is aware of the upcoming date. I refer to it as the 'sadiversary' and I start preparing for a sad day. I usually visit him with his kids at the grave site."

Especially during the first few years, the anniversary can be an occasion for sadness and reminiscing. But you should expect that this will happen. It is part of the grieving process, and the longer you were married, the longer you can expect that your life will be on pause that day. Take everything as it comes and above all, don't blame yourself for any difficult emotions or fresh grief you may feel around then.

DEALING WITH THE AWKWARD THINGS PEOPLE WILL SAY TO YOU

It's not just at work that people will say things that are awkward at best and inappropriate at worst.

But the fact is that you can't avoid this. No matter what, you will always have to deal with—and make allowances for—other people's issues. At various stages after your spouse's death, well-meaning friends and family members will say things that are not very helpful. Often, unfortunately, they are meant to be helpful.

For example, many people will advise you to "be strong."

"That didn't work for me," Julia, 52, said. "I think when they say this, they really mean 'We hope you will be strong.' But how does that help?" Julia says it would be much better to say: "Allow yourself to feel" or, "The worst feelings will pass."

In our culture, we want to say something to be nice and kind. "But people are really at a loss as to know what really would be nice and kind," Esther, 60, explained to us. "It would be better if they said something like, 'I'm at a loss as to what to say to you.'" This, she said, comes across as more honest and sincere.

> ## WHAT WIDOWS SAID
>
> You could also say: "Feel whatever you're feeling." Or, "You should know there are people who can help you lessen the intensity of your feelings."
>
> —EILENE, 60

People just don't learn what to say.

GENERAL ADVICE AND LESSONS FROM WIDOWS

The death of a spouse is one of the greatest traumas anyone has to face in life. Having come through this more or less intact, you learn things you can pass on to others.

For instance, Naomi, 28, says she learned something very important after her husband died in a tragic accident. "I learned that I am okay. And I will be okay. I know I don't handle loss well, but I found out that I can handle this and I can do it to honor him. I also learned that little things are important and, in the long run, memories are all you have when someone is gone. So you have to cherish those memories and think about them often."

Other widows said they learned that you never stop loving your spouse after they die. "You will never stop missing him," Callie, 36, said. "It just feels less intensely painful over time."

Brittany, 57, said she learned that routines are important. "Try and return to a routine as soon as possible," she said. "Stay busy, talk about it as much as you need to with people who love you and care about you, but structure your life with daily routines."

Caroline, 45, sums up what so many women said—or tried to say: "It's been almost two months since Joseph died, and all I can say for sure at this point is that I don't know how my life will play out. I've heard that time heals, but it doesn't erase. The shock of that day I learned that my beloved had left me still hits me like some form of PTSD. Joseph's death provided me with possibilities I never could have foreseen. I found ways to not be 'alone.' I make sure to get out of the house every day, make time to do fun things with my friends and, above all else, be with my family at every opportunity."

And many widows said they actually benefited in surprising ways from their spouse's death. They took on new jobs, started a foundation in his memory, or were forced to be more independent, which led their lives in new directions. Megan, 59, said: "I think through his death I found a greater purpose in my life."

Jocie, 65, said: "If nothing else, I've become more comfortable with death. It doesn't frighten me like it used to."

Widows experience many things they didn't expect. It would be great if someone could give you a heads-up about some of the things you will encounter. Typically they don't. As a result, you may feel like you are constantly being blindsided. As the title of this chapter suggests, only other widows can really help you to be somewhat prepared for the next close encounter with weirdness or some unexpected assault, and we hope that the advice some of them have provided in this chapter will help you cope with unexpected events that may intrude on your healing.

═ YOUR CHAPTER EIGHT TAKEAWAYS ═

- *Becoming a widow involves a transition. Expect that transition from wife to widow to be difficult. If everything goes well, it will end with you establishing a new identity, a new you.*

- *Few marriages are perfect. The failings in the marriage—especially those you learn more about after his death—can lead to heartache, pain, and rumination. Try to forgive your spouse and yourself for any pains from your marriage or partnership.*

- *Expect to experience a special kind of pain if your spouse was a substance abuser or an alcoholic, or was unfaithful. If you need to, talk to a therapist about your pain or fears regarding this to help you overcome them and heal.*

- *If the death of your spouse resulted from suicide, expect a more difficult recovery with special kinds of emotional hurdles.*

- *Some widows experience serious depression after the death of their spouse and may need therapy. If you feel you are experiencing this, seek out a professional who can help you work through it.*

- *Sometimes you may have to forgive your spouse—or yourself.*

- *Forgiveness of yourself may be necessary if you were a caregiver for your spouse as he was dying and you find that after his death you feel guilty that you could not save him.*

- *At some point, almost all widows think about dating, engaging in a sexual relationship, or getting remarried. Take some time to grieve your loss before dating or getting into a long-term relationship. Don't be afraid of using Internet sites to meet someone, but be cautious and wary of whom you are meeting.*

Remember to read Chapter Nine, "Your Game Plan." There you will find many checklists, charts, and forms that will be helpful as you transition to a new life.

chapter nine

your game plan

I was hoping for someone who had a plan laid out for me, a methodical plan I could follow. I needed an outline. When you're in this situation, you're just piecing it together. Everyone says, "Don't make any big decisions," and they're right, but there are a lot of decisions you just can't put off.

—ALICIA, 54

WHEN YOU SUFFER A LOSS, ESPECIALLY THE LOSS OF YOUR most intimate companion, you will have what we referred to earlier as "widow's brain." You will be disoriented, emotional, and feeling like you are in a constant fog. It will be difficult for you to focus on anything and a great challenge to keep track of things. You may find it stressful to even try and follow what is being communicated in a conversation. You cannot be expected to deal with everything a widow needs to handle in the first weeks, months, sometimes even years. You may be looking for direction, guidance, and assistance in getting through the painful times while still doing everything that needs to be done. Alicia said it very well: "I was hoping for someone who had a plan laid out for me." The widows we interviewed could have used that plan laid out for them.

We are calling that plan your game plan. And that's what this chapter is about. It offers you a game plan to deal with your grief, heal, and start to rebuild your life. It includes exercises, checklists, financial forms, charts, and other tools mentioned in the first eight chapters, collected here for easy reference. This chapter provides the structure you may need to handle social obligations, deal with legal complications, cope with financial issues, or just get through the first few years of widowhood.

If you are reading this right after your loss, we wish we could offer you complete reassurance that you will feel better soon and the fogginess you felt in the first days and weeks will go away in six months. But we can't do that. Everyone grieves differently, and everyone follows their own time frame for recovering from the death of a spouse. We certainly met a few women who were functioning quite well within six months to a year. However, many others were still in recovery mode two, three, four, or even five or six years later. Consequently, some of the aspects of the game plan in this chapter will refer to situations that might not come about for you for several years.

For example, dating and remarriage are two areas many widows face— often within the first two years after their spouse's death. Many widows we spoke with felt that others around them wanted them to begin a new relationship. However, they couldn't think of getting involved in a new romantic relationship for several years after the passing of their spouse. It might be four or five years before you allow yourself to think about dating again or getting remarried. Or you might be ready sooner than that. Either way, in this chapter, we have you covered. We will give you a checklist of considerations if and when you reach that point.

The tools and forms provided in this chapter will also help you assess your options in other areas, especially finances, and make appropriate decisions. Your game plan is a blueprint for the major areas of your life: household, child rearing, family, finances, and work. These tools can also be accessed online at Kristin Meekhof.com.

All widows know they must move on, but you may be held back by your grief and the emotions that are common in the year following a spouse's death. While no one can tell you what to do or how much you are capable of, the resources in this chapter can help you start to shape your future.

Part I. Immediate Concerns: Your Game Plan for the First Two Weeks

If your spouse has just died:

* If the death was sudden and unexpected, contact the necessary medical assistance and authorities.
* Call a friend, neighbor, or relative to be with you as soon as possible. As other loved ones arrive, have someone stay with you as much as possible.

Making funeral arrangements:

* Begin notifying family and friends, clubs and organizations. If you are providing transportation and lodging for people from out of state to attend the service, keep receipts of those expenses.
* Call your doctor and advise him or her of your loss. You might need a prescription to calm your nerves and help you sleep.
* If you and your spouse had preplanned funeral services, contact the funeral home or the memorial society. If not, decide on a memorial service and a final resting place for your spouse. Choose a local funeral home. Ask friends for recommendations.
* Create and publish an obituary. Funeral homes often assist you with this task.
* If your spouse was a veteran, no-cost burial arrangements and other benefits may be available for the funeral. The funeral director or a loved one can contact the Veterans Benefits Administration at 1-800-827-1000 or go online to www.va.gov.

- ❈ Make your wishes known for any service or memorial arrangements. Designate a friend or family member to keep track of the guestbook, donations, flowers, and cards. Have someone else take all phone calls and let you know who is calling.
- ❈ Order at least ten death certificates through the funeral director.
- ❈ Ask a neighbor, security service, or the police to keep an eye on your home while you are at the services.
- ❈ Take time for yourself and rest. Ask others to help you with things you need. Don't be afraid to ask—you need the help.

Handling the urgent matters:

- ❈ Contact your accountant or financial planner, if you have one, to review your cash flow and expenses.
- ❈ Be sure your bills will be covered for the next three to six months.
- ❈ Contact your estate planning attorney and/or trustee to begin whatever legal process is required.
- ❈ If you are not the estate executor or trustee, notify that person so an inventory of your spouse's property can be taken. Do not distribute any property or assets to any family or friends at this point.
- ❈ Begin collecting information so you can apply for various survivor benefits, such as Social Security, veterans' benefits, employee benefits, life insurance policies, and annuity contracts.
- ❈ If your spouse had a safe deposit box in his name alone, have the executor or trustee arrange to open it. This will require a copy of the death certificate, which takes time to obtain.
- ❈ Do not pay any bills incurred by your spouse out of your personal account. The estate is responsible for settling with all creditors. However, if there are bills such as a mortgage payment on your home, be sure these are paid. Discuss which bills should be paid versus which ones should not with your accountant, financial planner, or attorney.

Take care of yourself:

- ❋ Develop a daily routine devoted to your well-being. Exercise, meditation, yoga, and/or prayer are all soothing.
- ❋ Seek support from friends and family.
- ❋ Get plenty of exercise and work out regularly.
- ❋ Pay attention to what you eat and to making sure your nutrition is good.
- ❋ Get at least eight hours of sleep every night. Poor sleep routines and an inadequate amount of sleep have been associated with unhealthy life adjustment after loss.

Dealing with the necessities:

- ❋ Develop a to-do list: create a calendar for your Now, Soon, and Later lists.
- ❋ Open new accounts in your name before closing those of your spouse.
- ❋ Do not rush to tell banks, credit card companies, and other financial institutions about your spouse's death—they may freeze those accounts. You may lose rewards points as well.
- ❋ Review your own estate plan as well as assets and liabilities with your estate planning attorney and/or financial planner.
- ❋ Update documents and beneficiaries as necessary. Re-title joint accounts.
- ❋ Decide where to deposit various proceeds such as life insurance benefits and recurring income.
- ❋ Work with both your personal support team and professional advisors as you move through this period.

Remember:

- ❋ You are on a journey. The resting places and restarts are part of your path.
- ❋ Your journey does not end a year, or at any set amount of time,

after your spouse died. There's no finish line for grief. It may return when you least expect it. So be gentle with yourself.

Part II. Your First Month and Beyond Game Plan

Week Two To-Do Checklist

- ☐ If you have moved, even temporarily, notify utilities, newspaper delivery, your landlord, and the post office.
- ☐ Call your employer.
- ☐ Pay bills—mortgage or rent, credit cards, utilities, and so on.
- ☐ Open your mail.
- ☐ Locate your spouse's will and notify your attorney.
- ☐ Contact your children's teachers and/or schools.
- ☐ Order death certificates.
- ☐ File for life insurance benefits.
- ☐ File for Social Security survivor benefits for you and your children, if they are under eighteen.

Week Three To-Do Checklist

- ☐ Organize hospital, doctor, and other medical bills.
- ☐ Cancel insurance policies (such as your spouse's auto insurance) that you no longer need.
- ☐ Decide how to manage your husband's social media.
- ☐ Decide how to manage your incoming phone calls.

Week Four To-Do Checklist

- ☐ Prepare a list of people who need to receive acknowledgment of flowers, gifts, or condolences.
- ☐ Change the names on joint bank accounts and other financial assets.
- ☐ Maintain your sanity by:
  - ☐ Not being a people pleaser

- ☐ Not speaking negatively about yourself
- ☐ Trusting your gut
- ☐ Taking a breath
- ☐ Getting a notebook and each day writing down what you did to the best of your recollection
- ☐ Accepting help. You experienced a major trauma; you can't be expected to begin healing alone.

Ask for Help and Accept Help Checklist

The Things I Need Help With:

- ☐ Bring dinner over one night a week for the next month. (It is okay to be specific. Go ahead and ask for a certain day; then you will know that on Tuesdays, for example, you can count on not having to make dinner.)
- ☐ Keep me supplied with the basics: coffee, cereal, paper towels, toilet paper. (These staples are essential to have on hand, and it's easy to forget about them until you run out.)
- ☐ Help me write thank-you notes and cards.
- ☐ Pick up the ashes from the mortuary and keep them until I ask for them.
- ☐ Go on my spouse's Facebook page (and Twitter, LinkedIn, Pinterest, and so forth), and explain to his friends and contacts what has happened. Maintain the site for me for a month; then help me to decide whether to shut it down or continue it.
- ☐ Help me contact our bank, credit card companies, or other creditors and explain what's happened, close out accounts, or change the names on the accounts.
- ☐ Take over my duties as soccer coach for two months.
- ☐ Babysit my children one afternoon or evening a week.
- ☐ Help me with my daughter's (or son's) college application and/or financial aid application.
- ☐ Listen to my voice mail messages and call back people, relaying a message for me.

☐ Help me to go to my spouse's office and clean out his belongings.

☐ When I'm ready, help me go through the garage (or basement, attic, home office) and decide which of my spouse's things to keep and which to get rid of.

Go to KristinMeekhof.com, where you will find all the tools in this chapter in a print-ready format.

Part III. Your Social Support Game Plan

You will survive best if you have a support group. Here is your game plan for finding the social support you need:

* Support groups for widows are easy to find in most towns and cities. You can google "bereavement groups for widows," or you can contact a local mental health clinic or social service agency.

* To ease the burden of losing a husband, we recommend putting together a support team—an unofficial group of people you can call on for emotional support, financial or legal advice, practical assistance (for example, with yard work or babysitting), and just friendly chitchat. Your support team could include people to help you make decisions about work, confer about your children—their friends, schools, summer camps, or college applications—and plan your future. In fact, almost any aspect of your life might benefit from expert advice.

* While your support team may not be a formal group—that is, the members of the team may not know each other or ever meet as a team   you should still have a group of people that you recognize as your support team.

* Whatever your challenges, ask for help, seek support, or schedule a consultation with one or more members of your support team—particularly if you are faced with a big decision.

* Remember that when you are highly stressed, as you surely will be for at least six months and up to two or three years or more after your spouse's death, you should not make important

decisions on your own. And what would perhaps have been considered a small decision prior to your spouse's death may now feel like a major decision. Don't take it on alone.

YOUR SUPPORT TEAM MEMBERSHIP LIST
These Are My Go-to People For:

NEEDED SUPPORT	NAME	PHONE OR EMAIL
Emotional Support:		
Financial Support:		
Medical Support:		
Physical Support:		
Exercise Support:		
Entertainment Support:		
Other Support:		

Part IV. Your Legal Game Plan

Legal issues can be confusing and complicated. Most people don't understand the probate court. But to formally handle an estate, you must go through probate court. Here is your game plan to help you go through probate if you need to:

- ✳ File paperwork to handle your spouse's estate in probate court. You only need to go to the probate court or its website and ask for the appropriate paperwork to fill out.

- ✳ Make a list of the assets your spouse held in his name only. You may have to provide the probate court with a list of these assets.

- ✳ Publish in a local newspaper a notice to creditors to file any claims relating to debts your spouse may have had and for which the probate estate (not you personally) may be responsible. (Remember: if you were not a cosigner or the debt was not held jointly, they are your husband's debts, not yours).

- ✳ Inform interested parties, including all heirs, as to what is going on. Relatives, such as his children from a previous marriage or his parents, may be considered interested parties under the law and need to be informed that the estate is going through probate.

- ✳ Close the case once you have checked off and completed all items in this checklist. Once his debts have been paid from his estate and all interested parties have received their interest, you can ask the probate court to close the case.

- ✳ After twenty-one days (it may be longer in your state, so check on this), if no appeal has been filed, the case is officially closed.

Part V. Your Coping with Being a Solo Parent Game Plan

Guidelines for helping children cope:

- ✳ Encourage them to cry if they want to.

- ✳ Allow them to talk about their thoughts and feelings about their parent and the death.

- ✳ Express your own sadness openly; you might say, for instance, "I know you miss Daddy a lot. I miss him too."

- ✳ Acknowledge and accept their feelings. They will be more willing to talk openly if they are confident that whatever they feel will be acceptable to you.

❋ Don't dismiss or ridicule any feelings your child expresses. Mirror back their feelings ("I guess you are very angry sometimes about Daddy not being here"), which lets your child know you understand and that there's nothing wrong with their feelings.

❋ Don't forget the family pets. Dogs and other furry pets help establish connections with children in a way people cannot, and pets can help soothe a child's fears.

❋ Don't expect it to be easy. Talking to your child about the death of their other parent also means you are talking about the death of your spouse.

Checklist for Talking to Your Children about Their Father:

You will say the right thing most of the time if you keep the following guidelines in mind:

☐ Provide age-appropriate explanations of death.

☐ Reminisce about the good times related to your spouse; review family photos or videos, recall vacations, or talk about the fun you all shared at times.

☐ Openly express your love and support for your child; they need reassurance that they are loved.

☐ Don't hide your grief: you do have to be strong, but you can let them know that you grieve at times too.

☐ Explain your philosophical or religious beliefs and outlook. Your own philosophy or religious beliefs will be helpful to your child.

☐ Be honest with your child; you can let them know how you feel, but if they ask you a question and you don't know the answer, tell them you don't know.

☐ Kids needs normalcy and stability.

☐ Ask for feedback: if you are not sure whether your youngster is grasping something you are telling her, ask her what she thinks or if she understands.

☐ Know when your child may need professional help. If your child exhibits new and serious symptoms, such as aggressiveness, a drop in school grades, or extreme withdrawal for more than a few weeks, you should consider professional help with a child psychologist or a child therapist.

Guidelines for Disciplining as a Solo Parent:

- Trust your instincts.
- Be consistent.
- Set limits.
- Monitor your child closely.
- Be authoritative.
- Don't be afraid to make mistakes.
- Keep in mind that discipline is about a whole range of options, not just punishment.
- Maintain a sense of humor.

Seven Communication Skills Solo Moms Should Practice Daily:

1. Have an open-door policy.
2. Teach communication skills.
3. Have patience and be a good listener.
4. Use humor to reduce the tension in stressful situations.
5. Be responsive.
6. Be honest, especially about how you are coping with your own grief.
7. Be a positive communicator.

Part VI. Your Family and Friends Game Plan

If you are very stressed and it feels like family, relatives, and friends are not being supportive, try this four-step process to change the thoughts that cause you stress and anxiety:

Ask yourself the following questions and write down your answers:

1. Is it true that they hate me (or fill in any other negative thought that you are experiencing) and want to exclude me from friendship groups or family events? (If you answer yes, go to the second question. If you answer no, move to the third question.)
2. Do I absolutely know that it's true? (Answer yes or no.)
3. How do I react or what happens when I believe this thought?
4. Who would I be without the thought?

The next steps have to do with turnarounds. Turnarounds, according to Byron Katie, are opportunities to experience the opposite of what you originally believed. A statement can be turned around to the self, to the other, and to the opposite (and sometimes to "my thinking," when that feels appropriate).[2]

Find at least three specific, genuine examples of how each turnaround is true in your life, and then allow yourself the time and presence to feel them deeply. For example, if your concern is being left out of family functions or times your friends get together, your response to that first item may be: yes, it is true that they are excluding me from parties, movie dates, and celebrations. In doing the turnaround, restate each one and turn it toward you: "I am excluding them. I do this by failing to call them, avoiding their invitations, and remaining aloof." Continue doing turnarounds for all three items.

Part VII. Your Finances Game Plan

Locate the family financial records and assets:

Where to look:

  * ❋ Obtain a copy of your previous tax return.

---

2.   Adapted from Byron Katie's book *Loving What Is*.

* Check file cabinets, desk drawers, and safes.
* Contact your accountant or financial planner.
* Look on your husband's computer for passwords and financial files.

Determining your benefits:

* Go to the HR department of your husband's employer.
* Contact the Veteran's Benefits Administration (va.gov).

What Are Your Assets and Your Net Worth?

Here's how to calculate your assets and net worth:

YOUR NET WORTH

ASSETS	AMOUNT
Cash in checking accounts:	
Cash in savings accounts:	
Certificates of deposit:	
U.S. savings bonds (current value):	
Cash value of life insurance:	
Equity in pension, 401(k), and profit-sharing plans:	
Market value of IRA or Keogh plan:	
Surrender value of annuities:	
Market value of home or condo:	
Market value of other real estate:	
Market value of securities:	
Stocks:	
Bonds:	
Mutual funds:	
Other:	

ASSETS	AMOUNT
Current value of durable possessions:	
Autos:	
Home furnishings:	
Home appliances:	
Furs and jewelry:	
Precious metals:	
Collectibles:	
Recreational and hobby equipment:	
Loan receivables:	
Interest in a business:	
Other assets:	
TOTAL ASSETS:	
LIABILITIES:	
Current bills outstanding:	
Credit card balances:	
Car loans:	
Taxes due:	
Balance due on mortgage:	
Home equity loan balance:	
Other loans:	
Other liabilities:	
TOTAL LIABILITIES:	
SUBTRACT TOTAL LIABILITIES FROM TOTAL ASSETS:	
RESULT—YOUR NET WORTH:	

KEEP TRACK OF AND CALCULATE YOUR
MONTHLY AND YEARLY EXPENSES:

EXPENSE ITEM/ MONTH	JAN	FEB	MAR	APR	MAY	JUNE	JULY	AUG	SEPT	OCT	NOV	DEC
Mortgage/ rent:												
Utilities:												
Services:												
Home care:												
Insurance:												
Vehicles:												
Personal:												
Groceries:												
Education:												
Recreation:												
Entertainment:												
Medical:												
Child care:												
Pets:												
Charity:												
Savings:												
Gifts:												
Holidays:												
Loans:												
Taxes:												
Miscellaneous:												
TOTALS:												

Here is a form to help you create a budget:

BUDGET WORKSHEET

CATEGORY BUDGET	ESTIMATED AMOUNT	ACTUAL AMOUNT
INCOME:		
Wages and bonuses:		
Interest income:		
Investment income:		
Social Security or pension:		
Other income:		
TOTAL INCOME:		
INCOME TAXES WITHHELD:		
Federal taxes:		
State taxes:		
Local taxes:		
Social Security/ Medicare taxes:		
INCOME TAXES TOTAL:		
SPENDABLE INCOME:		
EXPENSES:		
HOME:		
Mortgage/rent:		
Condo fees:		
Homeowners insurance:		
Property taxes:		
Home repairs/ maintenance:		
Home improvement:		
UTILITIES:		

CATEGORY BUDGET	ESTIMATED AMOUNT	ACTUAL AMOUNT
Electric:		
Water and sewer:		
Gas:		
Garbage/trash:		
Phone (landline/cell)		
FOOD:		
Groceries:		
Eating out–Lunch:		
Eating out–Dinners:		
FAMILY OBLIGATIONS:		
Childcare/alimony:		
Day care/babysitting		
HEALTH AND MEDICAL:		
Health insurance (medical/dental/vision):		
Out-of-pocket expenses:		
Medication:		
Exercise/fitness (yoga/gym):		
TRANSPORTATION:		
Auto payments:		
Auto insurance:		
Auto maintenance/repair:		
Gas/oil/other:		
Other (subway, taxi, tolls):		
DEBT PAYMENTS:		
Credit cards:		
Student loans:		
Other loans:		

CATEGORY BUDGET	ESTIMATED AMOUNT	ACTUAL AMOUNT
ENTERTAINMENT/ RECREATION:		
Cable TV/videos/movies:		
Computer expenses:		
Hobbies:		
Subscriptions and dues:		
Books:		
Vacations:		
PETS:		
Food:		
Grooming:		
Boarding:		
Other:		
CLOTHING:		
New clothes:		
Cleaning:		
INVESTMENTS AND SAVINGS:		
401(k) or IRA:		
Savings account:		
Stocks, bonds, mutual funds:		
College fund:		
Emergency fund:		
TOTAL INVESTMENTS AND EXPENSES:		
SURPLUS/SHORTAGE (EXPENDABLE INCOME MINUS TOTAL INVESTMENTS AND EXPENSES):		

Red Light, Yellow Light, Green Light

In constructing your budget, which areas are red light, yellow light, or green light categories?

* Consider aspects of maintaining your home: write down the monthly cost of your mortgage, utilities, condo association fees, garbage collection, cable, homeowner's insurance, and needed repairs or maintenance.

* What are your other expenses? Write a list of your monthly and quarterly bills that will include auto insurance, cell phone fees, medical expenses, computer fees, car payments, and so on.

* What real estate or property taxes are you responsible for? Make a list. If you don't know what your taxes are, you can find out from your county assessor's office or recorder's office. You can usually get the information you need online. A good website to use is publicrecords.netronline.com. You will need the complete property address to obtain property data. Your taxes may be included in your mortgage payment, and you can determine this by reviewing mortgage statements for the past year.

* Exactly how much income do you have coming in each month? Do you know what money will be coming in? Is it income you can count on? Make a list of all steady income and total this amount.

* Add your total income. Add your total expenses. Using a calculator, subtract your monthly expenses from your actual monthly income. This will give you a true picture of your situation.

* Is your home your biggest expense? Do you have enough money coming in to continue living there? Ask yourself why you want to retain your home. Are you under pressure from family members to keep the house? Should you reduce costs by moving?

* If you can afford to stay in your home for a period of time, then put that decision on hold.

How Much Home Can You Afford?

CALCULATE HOW MUCH HOME YOU CAN AFFORD:

INCOME	PRE-TAX INCOME	AFTER-TAX INCOME
Salary:		
Other income:		
HOUSING EXPENSES	LAST YEAR	THIS YEAR
Rent/Monthly mortgage (including principle and interest)		
Property taxes:		
Homeowner's insurance:		
Maintenance:		
Other:		
TOTAL HOUSING EXPENSES:		
HOUSING EXPENSES AS PERCENT OF PRE-TAX INCOME:		
This percent should not be above 28%.		
TOTAL DEBT CALCULATION	LAST YEAR	THIS YEAR
Housing expenses:		
Credit card debt:		
Loan payments:		
Car loans:		
Other loans or debts:		
TOTAL DEBT:		
PERCENT OF PRE-TAX INCOME (DIVIDE TOTAL DEBT BY PRE-TAX INCOME):		
If your pre-tax income is no more than 36% of your total debt, you can likely afford your home.		

What should you transfer to your name:

- IRAs
- 401(k)s
- Brokerage accounts
- Bank and credit union accounts
- House or condo: Changing the house into your name is not necessarily an urgent matter, unless you plan to sell the house or condo and move.
- Automobile: His car should be transferred to your name; however, this is only important when it comes to selling the car.

Remarriage:

Think about these financial issues before getting remarried:

- Your children from your previous marriage: If you have children who are attending college on financial aid, your new spouse's assets may be factored into the expected family contribution and change your child's financial aid eligibility.
- Your adult children: They may have concerns about how a remarriage will affect their inheritance or the family structure in general. Discuss these issues openly with your children.
- Survivor benefits: If you rely on income from your late spouse's pension, Social Security, or veterans' benefits, find out whether you will be eligible to collect these benefits after a remarriage.
- Long-term care: Given the high cost of long-term care, having a partner who needs that level of care could strain both your bank accounts. If you get remarried, you would need to spend down both spouses' assets before either of you would qualify for Medicaid (even if you have a prenuptial agreement stating that certain assets be kept separate).
- Take care of yourself first: If you marry a man who has fewer assets than you, you may be jeopardizing your future security if you combine your assets.

Part VIII. Your Work and Career Game Plan

Facing questions when you return to your job:

If you work in any office or business where you interact with other people, be prepared for others to ask about your spouse and how you are coping with his death, and personal questions about you when you return to work. It is better to return to work prepared for the various well-meaning questions as well as those that are quite inappropriate or too personal. Having a few crafted responses in your mind may help you deal with the questions. Here are some suggestions:

- ✳ "Thanks for asking, but I'm doing just fine."
- ✳ "I appreciate everyone's kind sentiments and regards."
- ✳ "I needed to return to work to keep my mind off my sorrow."
- ✳ "You are so kind to ask about that, but I'm not ready to answer personal questions yet."

Determining Your Options If Your Current Work Is Not Likely to Provide an Adequate Income:

Here are some suggested options:

- ✳ Sell your house to reduce your expenses. Or move to a less expensive apartment or condo.
- ✳ Get a roommate, someone who could help with expenses.
- ✳ Move to a cheaper city.
- ✳ Change jobs or change careers.
- ✳ Consider going back to school for more education or training.

If you choose to try to change jobs or careers, read the next section.

If You Decide the Best Option Is to Seek a Job or Look for a New Position:

If you decide to look for a new job or a different career, here are some questions to help you understand your motivations and what you seek:

- What is my dream job?
- What can I reasonably handle?
- What types of work am I good at?
- What type of work environment is healthy for me?
- What type of supervision do I need?
- Is there any room for advancement at this company?
- Am I seeking this job so that I can gain experience and move to another company?

Are You Looking for a New Job?

Based on the advice we gleaned from career counselor Susanne Maurer and other career counselors, here are some basic ideas for beginning a job search:

- Look at job hunting as your temporary part-time—or full-time—job.
- Don't set your sights too high. It might be necessary to accept a lower-paying job (even a minimum wage job) to get yourself into the workforce or to get a foot in the door at a particular company.
- If you are a graduate of a college or a technical school, go back to that institution (even if it's been several years) and ask the alumni office or the college career center for help. Or ask about job fairs (which many college departments hold annually for undergraduates) so you can plan to attend.
- Consider applying for an internship.
- Network. Ask everyone if they know of any company that is hiring or anticipating a vacancy.
- Go to conferences, job fairs, workshops, and any other event where you can pick up a few tips and meet more people.
- Consider nonprofit agencies. They may be looking for someone with your skills.
- Volunteer at a business or agency where you would like to work. You won't make any money to begin with, but you

may be able to show them they really need you and should hire you.

* Sign up at a job placement firm or a temporary placement agency. You may only get short-term jobs, but you may also find a company and a job you really enjoy. And a company may find you and offer you a full-time position.

* Use social media. You may be skeptical about the practicality of social media; however, some social media sites can be very valuable when you are job hunting. LinkedIn, for instance, can extend your visibility around the country and with people and businesses you would never be able to contact otherwise.

What if You Have to Take a Job That Is Beneath You?

You may have to take a job you really feel is beneath you. However, even though your ego may take a hit if you accept a menial job, remind yourself (perhaps frequently) that you have taken a job for which you are overqualified for a good reason. Here are some reasons you can keep in mind when you are in a stepping-stone job:

* I took this job to get a fresh start.
* I accepted this position to build my résumé.
* I am only in this job temporarily to make financial ends meet.
* I am working here to get the job I really want.
* I am in this position to show myself that I am ready to return to work and that I will be able to handle greater professional responsibilities in the future.
* While I am in this position, I can always keep looking for another job.

Eight Lessons Kristin Has Learned in Pursuing a Second Career Following the Death of Her Husband

While pursuing a second career, Kristin has learned a few things that might help you if you too are pursuing a new career:

1. *Growth makes you vulnerable.* That means that rejection—which may be inevitable as you work toward a new career—will be especially tough. Just accept that it is normal to feel vulnerable at times.

2. *Follow your gut.* When your instincts tell you your direction is the right one, pay attention to that inner voice—not the outer critics.

3. *Check in with yourself.* Reassess your goals from time to time. Learn to adjust things as needed and have only one important goal at a time.

4. *Reexamine your game plan.* You may feel that your plan is solid, but as new challenges arise, you may need to readjust. Game plans sometimes need to change if they are not working the way you expected.

5. *Listen to your body.* Pursuing a new career can physically and emotionally deplete your resources, so be sure to rest and take care of yourself.

6. *Rejection happens.* Not only that, but you may feel it as another kind of loss. Don't dwell on rejection; keep your eyes on the ultimate goal.

7. *Gratitude.* I believe that gratitude is the answer to nearly every question. Be grateful and mindful of what truly matters.

8. *Dance.* Remember to celebrate each goal or finish line you cross. There will be several along the way. When you are able to do what you love most and experience joy, remember to dance!

IN CONCLUSION

We hope that this chapter was helpful to you as you work on your recovery. Keep in mind that even if aspects of the game plan aren't relevant to you now, they may be in the future. We planned this chapter as one you could come back to over and over as the circumstances of your life change.

We want to remind you once more that when the center of your life has changed with the loss of your spouse, it will take time to successfully cope with your grief. Don't place rigid and unrealistic expectations on yourself, believing that you have to be completely healed in one or two years, or even five years. Beating yourself up and being overly critical of your own decisions will not make the healing process any easier either. It may take several years to understand all that you've lost, heal from that loss, and begin to transform it into something positive for you. There is no finish line for grief, and it will not be over within a year. Learning to live with your loss will take time, and adjustments will likely be necessary along the way to help you cope. But you will cope and you will eventually heal.

We also hope that some of the stories of the women you met in this book will be a source of inspiration to you as you transform your life and fashion a new future for yourself. You are not alone and you can and will rebuild yourself and your life. Finally, be gentle with yourself and give yourself the gift of grace and beauty. We hope this book has helped you and continues to help you in your journey.

acknowledgments

OUR HEARTS ARE FILLED WITH GRATITUDE FOR ALL OF THE assistance we received from widows and experts in various fields, and the support from our close family and friends.

We didn't know when we started talking about a book in 2012 how long the journey would be. It seemed at times interminably long, what with interviewing widows, talking to many experts, working with an editor before the book was sold, and having the wonderful guidance and critical help of our agents, Anne Marie O'Farrell and Denise Marcil. They believed in the book right from the beginning, even when it was more a concept than a developed book proposal, and for that they have our gratitude.

We were fortunate along the way to receive support and encouragement from so many unexpected sources. One of the first people to contact us and express her support was Susan Toffler, whose own story of being widowed is told in this book. When we first heard from her in 2013, we began to have an inkling that our idea was going to resonate with women who have lost their husbands.

Soon after, we heard from Christie Coombs, whose husband died in the September 11, 2001, attacks on the World Trade Center. Ms. Coombs was generous with her time and met Kristin in Massachusetts.

Also, we have been most grateful for the early support of Carole Radziwill and Teresa DiFalco.

Over the years, we met several beautiful individuals who helped in various capacities. Akane Hebert offered support and encouraged Kristin to submit a blog to the *Huffington Post*. We also received support from Kris Schleder, Christine Isham, Lee Woodruff, Dr. Gary Hammer, Anna Rabe, the University of Michigan Adrenal Cancer Center, Deborah Francoise-Van De Vusse, Dr. Kathleen Rehl, the Honorable Lisa Langton, Jill Coney Daly, Katherine Siebenaler, the Honorable Elizabeth Pezzetti, Dr. Julie Kwon, Tajuana Anthony, Jolie Schiller Altman, and several other professionals who shared their expertise in our book. We had many friends who referred widows to us and talked to us (or, more often than not, listened to us) about the project. Vicki Rupert and Brad Axelrod were two—of many—such supporters. We thank you all!

More recently, Kristin had the opportunity to meet Lord Loomba, CBE, who founded and directs the international Loomba Foundation. This foundation supports and empowers widows and their children. Lord Loomba, CBE, invited Kristin to a special dinner at the United Nations in New York, where he was honored for his work.

We also have to mention the *Huffington Post*. They embraced Kristin as a writer by allowing her to share her story on their website. Because of the exposure Kristin got from her numerous *Huffington Post* pieces, she has been featured on many other websites. She is now a contributor to the *Shriver Report*—and we must thank both Lauren Schuette and Maria Shriver for welcoming Kristin as an Architect of Change.

Kristin is grateful for Dr. Deepak Chopra, for showing her how to live with an open heart and for introducing her to Mr. Poonacha Machaiah. Mr. Machaiah taught her about unbounded gratitude. And she would like to thank Wanda Long Walters, who made hospice in Kristin's home possible.

We are thankful to Ms. Kathy Tweitmeyer, Daffnee Cohen, and Peter Ricci for helping us develop Kristin's website. We are thankful to our first editor, Lynette Padwa, who gave us the benefit of her extraordinary abilities as an editor and as a widow herself to fashion a book proposal that would be appealing to a publisher.

And finally, a special, huge thank-you goes to Stephanie Bowen, our editor at Sourcebooks. When Stephanie first showed interest in this book, we knew we had someone extraordinary in our corner, someone who believed in the book and who let us know that she was just one person out of several at Sourcebooks who thought we had a wonderful concept. Stephanie helped in many instances to make sure we wrote what we wanted to write in a sensitive, compassionate way. She has also been extremely helpful in making sure the end result was a book we could all feel good about because we know it will help women for years to come. Shana Drehs became our second editor at Sourcebooks and she has been a wonderful addition to our team, as has our publicist Liz Kelsch.

appendix

resources for widows

IN THIS APPENDIX, YOU WILL FIND VARIOUS RESOURCES FOR widows, including those that we reference in the book. We hope these help you on your journey to healing.

WEBSITES OF KEY ORGANIZATIONS REFERENCED IN THE BOOK

- The Loomba Foundation, Caring for widows around the world: theloombafoundation.org
- The Desmond Tutu Peace Foundation: www.tutufoundation usa.org/2014/11/listening-to-the-story- of-grief
- The Social Security Administration: www.ssa.gov; www .socialsecurity.gov/survivorplan/howtoapply.htm
- Byron Katie's work: www.thework.com
- U.S. Department of Veteran's Affairs: www.va.gov
- National Career Development Association (to find a career counselor): www.ncda.org
- Deepak Chopra's website, which provides tools for healthy living: www.deepakchopra.com
- The Fetzer Institute, a website dedicated to activating and

celebrating the power of love and forgiveness as a practical force for good: fetzer.org/about-us

CHECKLISTS FOR FUNERAL PLANNING

* www.caregiverslibrary.org/portals/0/checklistsandforms_funeralplanningchecklist.pdf
* dying.about.com/od/funeralsandmemorials/ht/plan_a_funeral.htm
* www.caring.com/articles/caring-checklist-how-to-plan-a-funeral-or-memorial-service
* assets.aarp.org/www.aarp.org_/articles/foundation/aa66r2_care.pdf

GRIEF SUPPORT WEBSITES FOR CHILDREN AND FAMILIES

* http://www.aboutsandcastles.org

WEBSITES OF COUNSELORS, THERAPISTS, PHYSICIANS, AND COACHES USED AS RESOURCES IN THIS BOOK

* Pauline Laurent, CPCC: www.griefdenied.com
* Vicki Lind, MS: vlind.com/
* Susanne Maurer, career counselor and coach: www.dccareerservices.com/about-us.html
* Colleen Phillips, business and executive coach: www.piecestoprofit.com/about.html
* Jill Gafner, caregiving trainer: globaltrainingexperts.com/about.htm
* Christine Cantrell, PhD, psychologist: www.royaloakclinicalpsychology.com/about_us.html

✼ Irene Swerdlow-Freed, PhD, psychologist: www.drswerdlow -freed.com

✼ Steven Ceresnie, PhD, psychologist: www.stevenceresniephd .com

✼ Byron Katie, author and speaker: thework.com

BOOKS WE REFERENCED

✼ Jill Gafner: *Personal Positioning for the Caregiver*
✼ Joyce Carol Oates: *A Widow's Story*
✼ Byron Katie: *Loving What Is*
✼ Joan Didion: *The Year of Magical Thinking*
✼ Anne Lamott: *Help, Thanks, Wow*
✼ Mark Nepo: *The Book of Awakening*
✼ William Bridges: *Managing Transitions: Making the Most of Change* and *The Way of Transitions: Embracing Life's Most Difficult Moments*
✼ Julie Metz: *Perfection*
✼ Carol Staudacher: *A Time to Grieve*
✼ Earl Grollman: *Living When a Loved One Has Died*
✼ Marianne Williamson: *The Gift of Change*
✼ Kristin Neff: *Self-Compassion*
✼ Pema Chödrön: *The Places That Scare You* and *When Things Fall Apart*
✼ Debra Holland: *The Essential Guide to Grief and Grieving*
✼ Pauline Laurent: *Grief Denied: A Vietnam Widow's Story*
✼ Sally Balch Hurme: *Checklist for Family Survivors: A Guide to Practical and Legal Matters When Someone You Love Dies*

PROFESSIONALS WHO CONTRIBUTED TO THIS BOOK

✼ Rich Harter, Director of the Office of Evangelization at the John Paul II Center/Archdiocese of Milwaukee:

www.archmil.org/Year-of-Faith/Evangelization/A-New
-Commitment-to-the-New-Ev1.htm

* Jill Koney Daly, attorney and probate register: www.icle.org
/modules/About/bio.aspx?&Pnumber=P34380

* Dr. Kathleen Rehl, financial expert: www.kathleenrehl.com/

* Bryan Wisda, financial expert: bryanwisda.com

* Christine Isham, certified financial planner and president
of Northern Financial Advisers: findanadvisor.napfa.org
/Members.aspx/View/6760/4462

index

about the authors

Kristin Meekhof is a Korean American adoptee. Within days of her birth, she was abandoned on the streets of Seoul, Korea, and adopted by her parents, who lived in Michigan. When she was nearly two weeks shy of her fifth birthday, her adoptive father died from complications related to cancer.

Meekhof graduated from Kalamazoo College with a major in psychology and completed the master of social work program at the University of Michigan. She was widowed at age thirty-three. She contributes to the *Huffington Post*, MariaShriver.com, and the *Shriver Report*.

James Windell is an author, editor, and teacher. He is an adjunct faculty member in the criminal justice departments at Wayne State University and Oakland University. He was a court clinical psychologist with the Oakland County (Michigan) Circuit Court's psychological clinic for more than twenty-five years, where he conducted group therapy with delinquent adolescents and co-led a high-conflict postdivorce group. He was a weekly newspaper columnist for thirty years, writing about parenting issues. Among his twenty-five books are books about parenting, high-conflict divorce, postpartum depression, and criminal justice. He is the editor of the *Michigan Psychologist*, the newsletter for the Michigan Psychological Association. And his Childproof Parenting blog can be followed at jwind27961.com.